MODERN HEBREW POETRY

IOWA TRANSLATIONS

Contemporary Korean Poetry
Modern Chinese Poetry
Mihail Eminescu
The Poetry of Postwar Japan
Contemporary Yugoslav Poetry
Russian Poetry: The Modern Period
Modern Hebrew Poetry

General Editors
Hualing Nieh Engle
Paul Engle

MODERN HEBREW POETRY

Translated with Introduction by
BERNHARD FRANK

University of Iowa Press
Iowa City

LIBRARY OF CONGRESS CATALOGING IN PUBLICATION DATA

Main entry under title:

Modern Hebrew poetry.

   (Iowa translations)
    1. Israeli poetry (Hebrew)—Translations into English.
2. English poetry—Translations from Hebrew. I. Frank,
Bernhard, 1931-   II. Series.
PJ5059.E3M6   892.4'15'08   80-20037
ISBN 0-87745-106-0
ISBN 0-87745-107-9 (pbk.)

University of Iowa Press, Iowa City 52242
©1980 by The University of Iowa. All rights reserved
Printed in the United States of America

CONTENTS

Foreword   xv
Introduction   xix
On the Hazards of Translation   lix

Khayim Nakhman Bialik   1   Take Me Under Your Wing
                                Homecoming
                                A Twig Plummets
                                from At Evening Time
                                On the Slaughter
                                My Father
                                Message
                                from   In the City of Slaughter

Sha'ul Chernikhovsky   13   Vulture! Vulture in Your
                                Mountains

Zalman Shne'ur   14   Snow Song

Avigdor Ha-me'iri   15   Silence
                            That Very Night

Israel Efrat   17   *from*   Written in a Public
                                Restaurant
                            Interstice in the Deep
                            The Bird of My Being
                            Narcissus
                            Seashell
                            Certain Days
                            The Heart Will Have Its Way
                            Marine Biology

Uri Tsvi Greenberg   21   The Cutting Off

Esther Raab   22   "You are the man —"
                        "Like a bird dead in the stream"

"My arms are raised towards you"
"Today I am modest as a beast"
Self-Portrait
Etruscan Statue

Avraham Shlonsky   26   A Citizen's Dissertation on His
         Neighborhood

Miriam Yalan-Shteklis   27   *from*   Prayer to be Sung

Yokheved Bat-Miriam   29   "Just as You see me, that's how I
         am"

Levi Ben-Amittai   30   On a Fall Night
         My Soul in the Palm of Your Hand

Avraham Khalfi   31   The Digger for Gold
         In the Night Birds Fell
         A Certain Man
         Suburb
         "Flowers pink with ebony"
         "Tonight the moon fell"
         "A golden-green dawn"

Shin Shalom   35   Evenings, When Sparks
         Marvel Down . . .
         All's Not That Simple

Yonatan Ratosh   37   A Million

Natan Alterman   39   Red Ridinghood
         Summer Night
         Tonight
         The Foundling

Le'ah Goldberg   43   The Tree Celebrates the River
         Khamsin of Nisan
         From My Mother's House

Elul in Galilee
from   The Italian Poems:
          Heat Spell in Venice
          Open Window in Florence
On the Hazards of Smoking

Gavri'el Preil   47   Fishermen
Shining Thing
Lakes
Beyond the Imaginary Garden

Dov Khomsky   49   Sunbeams Diagonally
A Cloudless Morning
Your Eyes That Gaze
Paper Flowers
The Distance from Me to You
The Moon Dips in the Puddle's
    Flow
Even on the Loveliest of Nights

Shmu'el Shatal   53   Winter
Winter (alternate translation)
The Mountain's Side
Between You and Me

Zelda   56   Black Rose
Faint Echo
Here's a Woman Lived to an
    Extreme Old Age
An Enchanted Bird
The Merry Imagination
The Acacia Tree

David Roke'akh   59   The Fleeting Too
Childhood
Then
Every City
The Spring of Cities

Contents   vii

Amir Gilbo'a   61   Against the Wind
In the Dark
A Red and Blue Song
The Riders' Horses
"I pray from the heart a psalter"
"Me — I am but one . . ."
"After a thousand years . . ."
"I went out into that welcome
     cold . . ."
"I don't want to see black but"
"I put the tip of the pen to the
     paper . . ."

Abba Kovner   65   Observation on a Solitary Tree
This Way, This Way
Note Apropos the Neighbor's
     Garden
Observation on a Small Harbor
     Outside the Military Zone
Note Apropos a Light Breeze and
     an Elderly Couple on a Bench,
     Together, in the National Park
     at Ramat-Gan

Shlomoh Tan'ee   68   We Too
End of Summer
End Song

Benjamin Galai   70   Of the Travelers That Won't
     Come Again
From the North Pole
The Days of Sarah

Yekhi'el Mar   73   The Anglers
One Tiny Bird
That Street of Mine

Khayim Guri   75   His Mother

Odysseus
There Once Was a Dove
"I fancy that I'm standing
    guard . . ."

Yehudah Offen   78   "leaves"
"Air drips from rock"
Inwards

M. Winkler   80   "The sun held in tender hands"
Birthday
Conclusion
"Night after night I come to
    worship . . ."
"And so they withered"
At the Art Exhibit
"The evening closes over me . . ."

Aharon Amir   84   Stone
Cock
When It Came Time
Odeon
Exit from the Garden of Delights

Yehudah Amikhai   89   Of the Three or Four in the Room
For My Birthday
Defoliated Leaves
My Father
"Like two stones at the bottom of
    a slope . . ."
Both of Us Together and Each Apart
The Clouds Are the First Fatalities
"The diameter of the bomb was
    thirty centimeters"
"The old ice factory in Petakh
    Tikva"
"Early in the morning you
    lean . . ."

"For my beloved, combing her
   hair . . ."
"The people on this beach will
   never"

Anadad Eldan   98   Foam Blanches
The Candle of Brief Times
"Between the white stone canyons"
At Your Naked Back

Tsfrirah Gar   100   After the Guests Departed
First Rain
Only Statues Don't Shy Away
Seeing the Light
Tin Toys
Grown Old and Full of Years
Salt Statues
A Spot on the Sun
In the House at Midnight

Tuvia Rúbner   106   Sunflower
Spring in the Land
The Fire That in the Stone
My Father
"In the empty street every shutter
   is bolted"
Lullaby

Ben-Zion Tomer   109   Copy
Heartfelt Pity
Phantoms
Don Quixote

Avner Trainin   112   Sunbeams
Cat in the Dovecot
Ancient Song

Pinkhas Sadeh   114   The Angel

x   Contents

Dan Pagis 116 The Journey
Brothers
Autobiography
A Moment at the Louvre
Point of Origin
Hide and Seek
Impromptu Heart
The Elephant
Armchairs
Fossils
Balloons
Two-Legs

Mosheh Dor 124 Safety Pin
At a Loss
There's a Certain Difference in the
Air

Eli Netser 126 These Colors This Tune
My Best Clothes
This Fugitive Beauty
Looking at a Chagall Painting
The More
Star-Sown
Night Walk
Almond Blossoms

David Avidan 130 Cradle Song
Sleep, Leopard, Sleep
Domination as Another Form of
Weakness
Personal Problems
The Streets at Their Leisure Rise
The Spot Remained on the Wall

Itamar Ya'oz-kest 134 "Apples"
Yonder
On the River Lookout

Quarry
from   My Father — Is the Root
     "The flag on the house you
       dwelled in . . ."
     "A certain house buries"
     "I sit in the white light"
     "The hand — is the tree's"
     "The monuments"
     "— Where is the path,
       Father . . ."
     "What point . . ."
     "You build your house"
     "My father is the root in
       the earth"
from   Ordeal by Fire
     (The Bergen-Belsen
       Episodes)
     "Railway car"
     "Suddenly a squeal"
     Shot
     "The children called"
     The Funeral

Ori Bernstein   141   Silent Song
     Dog on the Road
     Another Time
     Conversations
     Departure
     Not for You

Yekhi'el Khazak   145   "All night long burned the bridges"

Daliah Rabikovich   146   Mechanical Doll
     The Dress
     Surely You Remember
     A Personal Opinion
     Portrait
     How Hong Kong Was Destroyed

Ya'akov Beser   153   Snake Skin
                            A Child Built a Castle
                            All the Caverns of Light
                            In the Beginning My Mother
                                Screeched
                            The Silence Plucks Chords
                            It Is the Silence

Mal'akhi Bet-Aryeh   158   Flesh from Flesh

Ya'ir Hurvits   159   For My Love Rising Early
                            On a Clear Night
                            Sorrow My Love

Me'ir Wieseltier   162   "Take poems, but don't read"
                            "I shall empty my head like
                                jam . . ."
                            +30° C
                            The Weather
                            Friends
                            "— And even if they live . . ."
                            Caution Prevents Accidents
Appendix   167   Notes on the Poets

FOREWORD

Theology once believed that "translation" could mean direct removal to heaven of the body without intervening death. All too often in being translated, a poem loses its life.

Literal translation of a poem into bare prose may help understanding of basic word meanings, but that is not the poem. The "meaning" of a poem lies in the emotional energy which the poet has added to the simple intent of the word. The poet is not giving a literal account of his life, but an imaginative one. This is why an imaginative person often gives a translated version which is closer to the poet's own intention than a so-called scholarly version.

The Iowa Translation Series is an expression of the International Writing Program, which brings "creative" writers from all parts of the world to write their own books in their own language, to learn other contemporary literatures as well as this country's farms, factories, arts and literature, and to translate their own work into English (with help from young American writers). They sometimes also translate their own country's contemporary writing, and often put the books of American writers into their own languages. Often a foreign writer in Iowa City will meet the American writer whom he has already translated and published at home. This recently happened to members of the International Writing Program who had translated Kurt Vonnegut into Polish and John Cheever into Danish. We found an American who had translated our Romanian poet.

In the dangerous twentieth century people of good mind and good will must translate or die. People must talk to each other; Poetry is the highest way of talking. Translating poetry is also talk, a dialogue between the two languages. To translate is one of the toughest jobs offered to the human race. It is also an honor, a privilege and, alas, a miserably rewarded labor. It is absolutely indispensable, in order to expand our aesthetic and emotional lives in a frighteningly shrinking world.

To look at a jumble of words in a foreign script, a wholly unintelligible page of ideograms, even words in our own Latin alphabet which give us no immediate meaning, and then to find a translation which proves that the poet of those original shapes of sounds was expressing emotions as intense as our own, and very similar! That reassurance of our common humanity we desperately need.

The International Writing Program tries to bring such understanding, especially from the rarer languages.

Surely there is no other example like Hebrew of a language brought back to daily, idiomatic life largely by the efforts of one man. The scattered Jews spoke scattered languages, but Eli'ezer Ben Yehudah, in what can only be called a frenzy of commitment to the ancient speech, brought the multiple-speaking Sephardic and Ashkenazy Jews together in using a shared Hebrew. It is a miracle that the Hebrew language survived the thousands of years of disuse. Any poem in any language is a miracle, but the most miraculous event we know is that poetry survived in a lost language.

In the Soviet Union's first year Hebrew was denounced as a "religious and bourgeois language," in a country with so many Jews. Not only were men and women attacked, but their own unique, valued words.

The new trend is a sharp irony — to use a language which once huddled in small communities, cut off from the nation around it, in an international way. Poetry is written now in a language once considered "dead," as this anthology shows.

One of the remarkable aspects of modern Hebrew poetry, written in a little country always waiting for invasion, is that most of the poems are personal. The daily tension of survival, the politics, the destruction, the fighting, seem to be almost deliberately ignored. The poet Zelda writes about the "evaporated" flesh of a very old woman that stirs "revulsion in corpulent men/and in the green leaves of the mulberry." Abba Kovner writes: "In the last seven leaves/I discovered ten shades of green." That was written in an environment not only of desert, but of plane, tank, gun. Yehudah Amikhai writes: "Thirty-two times have I entered life/And each time pained my mother less,/The others less,/ And me more."

In brief, in a country which survives by looking outward every second of each year for survival, we find a poetry of inward-looking. Tuvia Rübner says it all:

In the empty street every shutter is bolted.
Where did I come from? and where
am I going? The flanks
of the houses are gray in the scorching sun. Here's not

Where my house is. This isn't my street. My house
isn't here, the scorching sun
underfoot. No one's with me,
in all the street no man can give

Me an answer, one redeeming word . . .
— And suddenly the lurching car,
masked faces . . . a scream . . . and a pointed arm . . .
My God, my God, open a door for me.

That is, of course, a political as well as personal poem. In these
reckless and foolish times, the most private feeling and the most public
event are, tragically, one.

The translator of this book quotes John Ciardi's remark that "one can
be a poet only in the language in which one first said, 'Mama.' " Hebrew
poetry denies that. Most of these poets began by crying "Mama" in
another tongue.

Hualing Nieh Engle, Director
Paul Engle, Consultant
International Writing Program
School of Letters
University of Iowa

GENERAL EDITORS
IOWA TRANSLATIONS

GENERAL EDITORS'
ACKNOWLEDGMENTS

Special acknowledgment is made to the Northwest Area Foundation of
St. Paul (A. A. Heckman, former executive director, and John D. Taylor,
present executive director). The Foundation's grants have made many
books of translation possible in the International Writing Program.
Other foundations, private corporations such as Deere & Co., Exxon,
ITT, ATT, DeWitt Wallace Fund, Jurzykowski Foundation, have also
contributed. They recognize that today the people of this earth (is it
spinning too fast?) need each other, and that the poets of all countries,
in Chinese, Bengali, Urdu, Polish, Spanish, Arabic, Turkish, and
Hebrew, need each other.

By helping us bring the writers of the world to this small town, Iowa City, the University of Iowa proves its deep commitment not only to all the arts, including that neglected art, translation, but to the brilliant and suffering people who float on the surface of their floating continents. To support works of the imagination is itself an imaginative act.

INTRODUCTION

An Historical Overview

I

A single individual is credited with providing the main thrust of the revival of Hebrew as a spoken language. Eli'ezer Ben Yehudah (1858–1922), a frail, consumptive man with an iron will, discovered the conversational potential of the language while socializing with a Hebrew-speaking intelligentsia in Paris. He was again impressed, in Algiers, at the fluency with which the Jewish community there spoke the language of the Bible. Once settled in Palestine, he directed all his energies towards the fulfillment of his dream: the reestablishment of Hebrew as the spoken language of Jewry at large.

A problem in the Palestinian school system turned out to work in Ben Yehudah's favor. The Ashkenazy Jews of Central and Eastern Europe spoke the Judeo-German Yiddish; the Sephardic Jews of Spanish, Turkish, or Arabic origins either spoke Ladino, which was much like Yiddish but with Spanish instead of German as its base, or else they spoke Arabic. Since the Ashkenazy parents adamantly refused to have their children educated in Ladino (Arabic never really coming into consideration) and the Sephardic parents refused to have their offspring educated in Yiddish, a common language was sorely needed. What language would be more apt than the one in which the Jews already performed their religious rites, namely Hebrew?

Eli'ezer Ben Yehudah had his way in the education of the boys; yet Jewish women were forbidden to speak or even learn Hebrew. To bring the boys up in one language and the girls in another was clearly senseless. And so, putting logic before tradition and defying rabbinical opposition, Ben Yehudah established separate schools for the girls; instruction was in Hebrew.

Nor was Ben Yehudah content with the conversion of the young. Both his wife and son were permitted to speak no other language, and his circle of friends was literally coerced into conversing with him in Hebrew only. As what had seemed impossible was slowly becoming a reality, Ben Yehudah, in 1910, began compiling his *Milon,* or dictionary (he derived the word from *milah,* "word"). Wherever feasible, he garnered and defined the vocabulary of the past: from the Bible, the

Talmud (or Oral Law, of the post-Biblical period), and the works of the medieval Spanish writers. Where no words were available, however, for a particular sense, Ben Yehudah did not hesitate to adapt obscure or outdated Biblical terms to new uses. He also borrowed from other languages, always imposing the Hebrew grammar on the words either by use of the proper prefix or suffix, or by subjecting the words to the proper conjugations. And when neither adaptation nor borrowing filled the need, he simply invented. Some of his coinages did not take root and dropped out of the language by and by; yet many others are now firmly ensconced. The bulk of Ben Yehudah's *Milon* appeared during his lifetime; a group of scholars completed the task after his death.

Eli'ezer Ben Yehudah had also helped found the *Va'ad Ha-lashon* (Council of the Language) to preside over the formidable task of keeping Hebrew up to date while preserving its purity. Today that task is carried out by the Academy of the Hebrew Language.

Ben Yehudah's efforts met some severe setbacks as well, most notably the attempt in 1914 to make German the language of instruction at the Technicum in Haifa. Happily by then the *Yishuv* (or settlement) had taken Hebrew to its heart and remonstrated violently; the Techinicum had to give in. When in 1918 the cornerstone of the Hebrew University was laid, there was no longer any room for debate; instruction was to be in Hebrew.

Precisely because Hebrew was *not* a dead language, precisely because Ben Yehudah was able to observe several, albeit modest, models of Hebrew-speaking communities, was he encouraged to pursue his dream. And indeed Hebrew had never, since its inception in pre-Biblical days, ceased to be spoken. After the exile from Jerusalem to Babylon (485 B.C.E.) when Aramaic competed with Hebrew and infiltrated its vocabulary, the Jews did not, according to most present day scholars, cease to speak the language of their fatherland. And although following the destruction of the Second Temple in 70 C.E. the number of Hebrew speakers was indubitably badly depleted, it has been shown that the language of the Mishna, that part of the Talmud which was written in Hebrew, was not confined to literary uses only but remained the language of the populace at large.

Only the large Jewish community in Alexandria abandoned Hebrew first in favor of Aramaic, then to speak a Greco-Judaic vernacular similar to Ladino and Yiddish, with Greek as its base. Consequently, the

Alexandrian Jewish community was almost entirely assimilated by the fifth century. The Babylonian Jewish community, on the other hand, which had gone on speaking Hebrew, survived several more centuries; and when persecution drove it out, its scholars took with them the vestiges of their culture and ultimately were major forces in bringing about the Golden Age of Hebrew culture in Spain.

Although proof is at times spotty and hypothetical, backed up by anecdote and legend, it is generally held that Hebrew continued to be spoken in some pockets of Jewry, though not necessarily the same ones, uninterruptedly up to the present. One of the great advantages of Hebrew was that it provided a common language for travelers and the communities they visited and allowed for cultural exchanges between them. Eldad the Danite, of the ninth century, thrilled Jewish audiences all around the Mediterranean with his tales of the Lost Tribes of Israel. Passing his tales off for fact, he maintained that the tribes spoke Hebrew exclusively and, as proof, claimed to speak no other language himself. The messianic pretender David Re'ubeni similarly claimed, upon arrival in Italy from Arabia in 1524, that he spoke only Hebrew. Clearly both men must have found a Hebrew-speaking audience, or their monolingual claims would have fallen on deaf ears.

If the spoken language was never altogether dead, the written language was at all times very much alive. Biblical explication, moral law, philosophy, and science, as well as literature, were mostly written in Hebrew. The locale of the writings of course shifted with the fortunes and wanderings of the Jews; yet wherever they went they wrote, and most of what they wrote was in the language of their religion and their homeland.

II

The Bible is the oldest surviving piece of Hebrew literature, faithfully preserved in form and stunning in its impact on the world at large; yet it was not the only book written during that long period of its compilation from as early as the thirteenth through to the second century B.C.E., nor was it the first. In the 1930s excavations in Syria brought to light the Ugaritic tablets containing poems antedating the Bible, written in a language similar to Hebrew, and employing similar poetic techniques. And the Biblical Hebrew, too, reveals evidences of Egyptian, Akkadian, and Canaanite linguistic influences. The Bible, furthermore, mentions over a dozen titles of books contemporaneous with it; that these have failed to survive is hardly surprising. It took the fanatic devotion of the Jew for his Book of Books to ensure its preservation over centuries of repeated persecutions and migrations.

Hebrew poetry makes its debut inauspiciously in the fourth chapter of the Book of Genesis. In the midst of a genealogical count-down, Lemekh, a direct descendant of Cain, suddenly bursts into song for the benefit of his two wives. Barely longer than a nursery rhyme, the poem is nevertheless strangely violent:

Adah and Zilah listen to my voice
wives of Lemekh pay heed to my speech
for I have slain a man who would injure me
and a child for striking me.
For seven-fold avenged shall Cain be
and Lemekh seventy-fold and seven.

(Genesis 4:23–24)

Violence, or more specifically war, is the occasion for several other early Biblical poems. Moses and Deborah celebrate at some length their triumph over the hosts of Pharaoh and the Canaanites respectively; conversely, David laments the victory of the Philistines and introduces, for the first time, a personal note near the end as he addresses his slain comrade:

I grieve for you my brother Jonathan
very pleasant have you been to me
more wonderful was your love to me
than the love of women.

Yet David recollects himself almost immediately, and the lament concludes as it had begun, on a rhetorical note:

How are the mighty fallen
the weapons of war perished.

(2 Samuel 1:26–27)

A number of short poems fall into different genres. Thus Joshua's command during the battle for the Holy Land:

Sun, in Giv'on halt,
and moon in the Valley of Ayalon!

(Joshua 10:12)

which employs an assonantal rhyme, *dom*/Ayalon. Thus, too, the riddle with which Samson challenges his Philistine guests:

From the eater issued edibles
and from the bold sweetness

to which the answer was:

What is sweeter than honey
or bolder than a lion.

(Judges 14:14, 18)

Isaac's blessing of Jacob whom he mistakes for Esau, besides containing rhyme (*Amím/le'umím*) and what in Hebrew would be considered only weak rhyme (*Akhékha/imékha*), also contains balance and antithesis:

Be he who curses you accursed
and he who blesses you blessed.

(Genesis 27:27-29)

Both the range and frequency of the poetry increase in the later books of the Old Testament: the moral strictures, forebodings, and laments of the prophets; the hymns to God in the Book of Psalms; the "Anything you can do I can do better" speech of God in the Book of Job; and those two famous sources of embarrassment — the erotic Song of Songs and the pragmatic Ecclesiastes. In fact, both of these latter works were included in the Biblical canon only after much controversy. Lines such as:

How lovely, delectable you are, Beloved, in love-making.
Your stature is that of the palm, and your breasts
        resemble the clusters of the grape.
And I said, let me scale the palm and grasp its fronds,
And let your breasts be like the clusters of the grape,
        and the scent of your breath like apples.

(Song of Songs 7:6-8)

sent Jew and Christian alike into hasty pursuit of allegories wherein the beloved becomes either Zion or Christ. And the Preacher's "Eat, Drink and Be Merry" philosophy had Biblical editors intersperse the text of Ecclesiastes with many a "Trust in the Lord."

III

That for a period of one thousand years following the close of the Biblical canon no secular poetry of the order of the Song of Songs and Ecclesiastes can be found does not *necessarily* mean that none had been written, only that none had survived. Given human nature, it would seem likely that the Jew, like all men, went on singing and celebrating the profane as well as the divine. It is the low repute accorded such poetry by the rabbinate which may have assured its hasty demise. What is more ephemeral, by way of analogy, than the best sellers in our own present day culture? On the other hand, much liturgical poetry written during that same period is still extant even if many of the poets' names have been lost.

The poems took the form of penitential works (*shlilah*), elegies (*keenah*), and prayer-like verses called *piyutim* (from the Greek *poein*, which is the root of "poetry" as well). The most famous of the *paytanim*, or writers of *piyutim*, was the seventh century Palestinian Eli'ezer Kalir. Much admired by earlier ages, Kalir's opus is now regarded as verbose, contrived and overly learned. He employs the Biblical verse techniques, including acrostics of the letters of the alphabet and of his own name, a precedent the medieval Spanish poets were to follow assiduously.

When the Moslem Berbers led by Tarik invaded Spain at the beginning of the eighth century, they liberated the many Jews whose ancestors had come there after the destruction of the Second Temple, and who, in the last decade of the seventh century, had been enslaved by the Visigoths. Recognizing them as useful allies, the Moslems appointed the Jews guardians of the newly conquered territory. Many more Jews, having escaped persecution in Babylon and traveling through North Africa in the wake of the Berbers, crossed the Straits of Gibraltar and settled in Spain. Thus Hebrew culture not only revived but began to assimilate whatever it found attractive in the new conquerors' culture as well.

Soon the Jews of Spain were not only conversing in Arabic but were also writing their philosophical and scientific treatises in that language. And although the nature of liturgical poetry demanded that it be written in Hebrew, the poems' titles were often in Arabic. Furthermore, while the Arab poets sang the glory of the cities of Spain, their Hebrew confreres imitated their devices to celebrate the glory of Zion.

A typical and outstanding example of the poetry of the "Golden Age of Spain" is the work of the most famous, best loved, and critically most admired of the Hebrew Spanish poets, Yehudah Ha-Levi (ca.1075–ca.1141).

A physician by profession, Yehudah Ha-Levi nevertheless had very clear priorities:

HEAL ME, O LORD

(Written upon taking his medicine)

Heal me, O Lord, and I shall heal
Or if You deny me, I perish.
My drugs and concoctions are Yours, whether
For better or worse, or potent or weak.
Yours the decisions and never mine
On Your opinion rest both foul and fair.
Not on my medicinal arts do I rely
But seek Your healing powers everywhere.

The Spanish poets did not hesitate to write secular poetry, including love poems (some of these to members of their own sex); yet, perhaps because of Yehudah Ha-Levi's religio-patriotic fervor, his secular poems often lack conviction:

WHY LET THE SUN RISE

Why let the sun rise, why give it a glance
Once Myrtle has made her entrance?
She shames the sun with the glow of her beauty,
In their chores disrupts the heavenly legions,
Has declined to live in the upper regions
And transforms the myrtle into her canopy.

The play on the name Myrtle and the shallow hyperboles reduce the poem to a clever exercise. It is Ha-Levi's intense love for his God and Zion which forms the *idée fixe* of his work and which sings out most profoundly:

MY HEART IS IN THE EAST

My heart is in the East and I at the ends of the West.
   How shall I taste the food I eat and how can it please?
How shall I fulfill my vows and abstinence while
   Zion's in the grip of Edom and I in Arabia's chains?
As easy for me to abandon all the plenty of Spain as
   It is dear to me to behold the debris of a shrine.

Yehudah Ha-Levi suited action to song and when already in his sixties abandoned the plenty of Spain and began the perilous voyage to the Holy Land. Although we know that he had reached the Jewish communities in Egypt, his traces thereafter are blurred. Legend has it that he arrived by the gates of Jerusalem, sank down to kiss the ground while reciting his very long and famous poem "Won't You Inquire, Zion, after the Welfare of Your Captives," and was promptly trampled to death under the hoofs of an Arab rider's horse. Skeptics point out the legend's faulty logic, but, since no proof to the contrary has been found, the romantics persist with their tale.

Other much admired Hebrew poets in Spain were Shlomoh Ibn Gabirol (ca.1021–53+), Mosheh Ibn Ezra (ca.1055–?), and Avraham Ibn Ezra (ca.1092–1167). The golden age of Hebrew poetry lasted from 1000–1200 C.E.; with the Christian conquest of Spain and its attendant persecution, forced conversions, and ultimate expulsion of the Jews, the flourishing of Hebrew culture generally came to a halt. Once again the center of learning and literature shifted, this time to Renaissance Italy, Provence, and Sefed (*Tsfat*) in Palestine, where mystics and poets alike kept the Hebrew arts and letters alive.

Golden ages tend to cast leaden shadows, and the glitter of the Spanish poets gave rise to a long sequence of imitators in Italy. The least derivative of these was Immanu'el Ha-Romi (Immanuel of Rome, ca.1270–1330) who was acquainted with Dante and introduced the sonnet form into Hebrew poetry. Considered an "obscene" poet in his day because of his ambiguously erotic interpretations of Biblical tales, his works were banned by the rabbinical code, the *Shulkhan Arukh*. Less controversial and less original poets in Italy were Mosheh di Rieti (1388–ca.1460), who wrote a long Dante-esque poem in terzets, Azariah de Rossi of Mantua (1514–78), Leo da Modena (1571–1648), who composed pastorals, Mosheh Ben Mordekhai Zacuto (?–1697), and, most notable among the Italian poets and sometimes called the father of modern Hebrew, Mosheh Khayim Luzzato (1707–47).

Mosheh Khayim Luzzato wrote pastoral verse dramas — allegories celebrating the beauty of nature, love, and friendship. He was, however, excommunicated from Jewry because of his messianic pretensions. On a pilgrimage to the Holy Land he and his family contracted the plague and died. The modernism attributed to his works may stem from his theoretical writings about Hebrew poetics and from his depiction, if not prediction, of the ideal future Jew.

Thus had the torch been passed from cultural center to cultural center, and from century to century; three years after the death of Luzzato, in 1750, Moses Mendelssohn published the first Hebrew periodical, *Kohelet Musar,* in Germany. The gateways to the *Haskalah,* or Enlightenment, were about to be opened.

IV

Although the first Hebrew periodical failed, a second, *Ha-me'asef,* sprang up in 1783 and lasted till 1811; it readily became the mouthpiece of the *Haskalah.* A natural offshoot of the European Enlightenment movement at large, the *Haskalah* presumed to endorse whatever reason corroborated and to reject all else. The chief impetus was given the movement by the recent emancipation of the Jews in Western Europe. With civil rights at last accorded them, the notion took hold, especially among the Jewish merchant class, that the only barrier towards true acceptance by the Gentile world hinged on their readiness to assimilate. Obliterating the Jew's distinctiveness, overcoming his separatist way of life, appeared to be the key to easy integration, and *Khokhmah* (knowledge) was the ready means to that end. The equivalent of a college education, the study of science, history, languages, and literature, *Khokhmah,* it was hoped, would at long last end the medievalism of ghetto life.

Later critics, often overly threatened by the assimilative aims of the *Haskalah,* accused the *Maskilim* (the Enlighteners) of endangering and even betraying the Jewish identity. Yet, paradoxically, without the introduction of a liberal education, without the mental emancipation from the fetters of traditionalism, no Zionist movement could ever have been born. For, although, as in the wake of other liberation movements, a frantic scrambling for self-advancement sometimes ensued, and although some Jews assimilated so thoroughly as to leave the fold altogether, the return of Jewry at large into the mainstream allowed it to rediscover its potential, both mental and physical, in coping with a world of change. From a morbid preoccupation with Biblical explications it turned to the study of science and secular literature.

To disseminate its propaganda the *Haskalah* hit upon Hebrew as the only feasible medium of communication. Because the intelligentsia regarded Yiddish as a despicable mutilation of German, the *Maskilim* would not deign to use it; yet Yiddish, and *not* German, was the only language the Jewish people understood — with the exception of Hebrew, which, though they did not speak it, they employed faithfully in their religious studies. Hebrew then was revived for secular use not in fulfillment of a Zionist dream but merely out of pragmatic considerations; it was a "respected" language and as such was bound to find an audience for *Haskalah* propaganda. Inadvertently, however, the pragmatic and opportunistic promotion of Hebrew gave it its first major impetus towards rebirth as a spoken language.

Spreading beyond Italy, Hebrew literature began to appear in Germany and Holland ca. 1730, in Austria and southwest Russia ca. 1810, and finally in Russia proper by 1840. The *Haskalah* movement in Eastern Europe, however, was far more subdued than in the West, since the political emancipation of the Jews there had to await the Revolution of 1917.

Haskalah literature, like all propaganda, tended to be mediocre by dint of its preachments and imitativeness, and few names come down to us as authors of the first magnitude. In poetry Samuel David Luzato (1800–65) may deserve mention for his two volumes of Hebrew verse, *Kinnor Na'im* (The Pleasant Viol), and some of the satiric poems of Yehudah Lev Gordon, the poet laureate of the *Haskalah* (1830–91), are still amusing to read today. All in all, the *Haskalah* period led to the resharpening of a language dulled from disuse; the ground was being readied, ploughed, and enriched for the springing up of modern Hebrew literature.

V

In 1892, the year of Y. L. Gordon's death, a song, "To a Bird," appeared in the anthology *Ha-Pardess* (The Orchard), written by a young man of the Odessa group of poets, Khayim Nakhman Bialik. The king is dead, long live the king. Bialik (1873–1934) was received fondly from the very first by the Jewish reading public and was presently adopted as *ha-meshorer ha-le'umi* (the national poet). Bialik's fusion of private and public themes is usually put forward as the key to his popularity. When he sang of his own poverty, of his own love, the public not only identified with him but sensed broader, national implications.

Much of Bialik's early work deals with his childhood: the poverty of his family, its ghetto mentality and extreme orthodoxy, the early death of the father. These memories, as in the poem "My Father," are imbued with a deep affection and a sense of guilt for having been too young and powerless to help.

Following the pogroms of 1903, however, the tone of Bialik's work and his attitude towards ghetto life change drastically. Rage to the point of hysteria permeates some of his best known work of that period, a rage directed less at the persecutors than at the passive Jewish community that suffered and went on praying. The passivity of the herd had become intolerable to Bialik, and in his "In the City of Slaughter," for example, he lashes out against it.

The rage and intolerance became alleviated with the growth of the Zionist movement; hope began shaping into a reality, and the poems of Bialik's last period tend to be accepting, calm, literary. "The Pool," depicting a forest pool and the changes it undergoes with time and weather, is a well-known example from that period. Although the poem is naturalistic, critics here too insist on a national parallel which, however, hardly enhances the quality of the work. National adulation, in fact, seems to interfere with an objective assessment of Bialik's work. A minor poem like "A Twig Plummets" has been given several layers of meaning. The twig fallen from its mother-tree represents, we are told, Bialik's forthcoming poetic silence, represents poets generally, represents the Jewish community divorced from its homeland, represents, finally, man at large in his mortality. Yet the image of a fallen twig, like that of a fallen leaf, is too derivative to even rate the name of symbol. The charm of the poem lies in the petulant tone and the lilting rhythms; intellectually it is merely banal.

Idol worship has led to a reaction, and the younger generation of Israelis prefers the voice of later, more direct poets to the grandiloquence and pathos-cum-bathos of Bialik. Nevertheless, no poet writing in Hebrew today can be free of Bialik's influence any more than an English-language poet can be free of the influence of Shakespeare. Bialik is in the blood; inculcated into the mind of school children, he is memorized and quoted. Even the rebel-poet must, at least unconsciously, follow in the national poet's footsteps.

Bialik's impact on the generations following is the more remarkable since his work is not read now as it was meant to be read. Bialik wrote using the Ashkenazy pronunciation of Central and Eastern Europe; its stress falls on the penultimate syllable of a word. Israeli pronunciation however follows the Sephardic custom of the Spanish and Arabic Jews, stressing the ultimate syllable. The resulting metrical discrepancies have a parallel in the poetry of Chaucer. Before it was understood that the final "e" in the Middle English was pronounced, Chaucer had the reputation of being a poor scanner; the same charge could unfairly be lodged against Bialik. And he never did change over to writing in the Sephardic pronunciation, for once he came to Palestine in 1924, he ceased writing poetry. Many an explanation has been offered for this silence, usually attributing it to a conscious design on the poet's part. It is demonstrated, too, that Bialik still had the *talent* to write. Yet it would appear most in keeping with the elusive nature of the muse that although the poet still had the *ability* to write, the creative *drive* had simply abated. One is only a poet, it has been said, up through the time of one's most recent poem.

Two other names are usually grouped with Bialik; the three are heralded as the great triumvirate of the revival of Hebrew poetry. Yet the work of Zalman Shne'ur (1887–1959) has never been heartily adopted by the Israeli educatonal curriculum, and its influence, consequently, has been limited. Sha'ul Chernikhovsky (1875–1944), on the other hand, remains a major force in the development of Hebrew poetry. Not a product of the ghetto milieu of Bialik, Chernikhovsky studied medicine in Germany and was a practicing physician during his Palestinian years. His work was heavily influenced by the classics, and his translations of *Iliad* and *Odyssey* were a landmark in closing the gap between a Jewish-parochial and a universal mentality.

Although Chernikhovsky's poetry is driven by a syntax both forceful and pleasing, it is less impassioned, less involuntary than Bialik's. His famous long narrative poem "Baruch of Mayence," wherein he deals with Jewish persecution, has some of the hysteria of Bialik's middle period yet rings melodramatic rather than heartfelt; the plot, too, of the father murdering his daughters to prevent their being raised in a convent and then setting the whole town on fire smacks of Grand-Guignol. Unlike Bialik, Chernikhovsky continued to write poetry in Palestine, and his "Vulture! Vulture in Your Mountains" is addressed to its rugged terrain.

VI

Bialik, Chernikhovsky, and Shne'ur were primarily poets of the Diaspora. The generations that followed them, however, relinquished their roots in the foreign soil; they became known as the Palestinian Poets.

The early migrations to a Palestine ruled under a British mandate, came in three distinct waves: The First *Aliya* (or Ascension) occurred around 1890, in the wake of Russian pogroms. The Second *Aliya*, at the beginning of the twentieth century, was sparked by the spirit of the Russian Revolution of 1905; and the Third, postwar, *Aliya* was again triggered by persecution. The Communist regime established by the Revolution of 1917 had declared Hebrew a religious and bourgeois language and forbade its use in Russia. Eminent writers were jailed, and only through the personal intervention of the author Maxim Gorki was Lenin prevailed upon to grant them permission to emigrate.

The spirit of pioneerism (*Khalutsiut*) was infectious and wooed erstwhile diaspora writers like Uri Tsvi Greenberg away from lament, rebellion, and preachment to poetry of compassion and exultation. Religious concerns were replaced by the secular and writers' use of the Ashkenazy pronunciation gradually, and sometimes painfully, abandoned for the Sephardic.

In a time of joyous idealism a propagandistic poetry was inevitable. The *Kibuts* poets glorified manual labor and the homeland soil. Levi Ben Amittai, Benjamin Tannenbaum, Jehoshua Babinov, and Fania Bergstein belong to that group; like most propagandistic poetry their work held up only as long as the spirit of their time. Alongside them appeared *Meshorerey Hamoledet*, the Homeland Bards, including I. Z. Rimon, Rachel (Blaustein), and D. Shim'oni. These were mostly Second *Aliya* poets who sang the joys of the new land. Although hardly innovative, their scope was wider than that of the *Kibuts* poets, and they succeeded in simplifying the more cumbersome, if majestic, measures of Bialik and the Bible. Rachel (1890–1931), for instance, pioneered the writing of poems in the colloquial Hebrew and simply and movingly sang both of her love for the land and her private sorrows.

Alongside these two "naïve" schools rose a quite different group which one might call the Urban Sophisticates. Moving counter to the collective spirit of exuberance, looking inward and downward, were such artists as Avraham Shlonsky, Natan Alterman, Le'ah Goldberg, and the already mentioned Uri Greenberg. Their literary influences came from Western Europe: Freud, the French *Symbolistes,* and the German Expressionists. These artists found that they could not ignore the anxiety of the individual amidst the pioneering enthusiasm of their day. Thus, Avraham Shlonsky in his "A Citizen's Dissertation on His Neighborhood" deals with the boredom and despair of urban living. Alterman's "Tonight" delves into the estrangement of a couple — the lack of fulfillment, either physical or emotional, of one lover by the other. And while Le'ah Goldberg sang glowingly, lyrically (though not sentimentally) of nature and of love, she never espoused any national causes.

VII

In the late nineteen forties and early fifties it was to these Urban Sophisticates with their sense of style and irony, their no-nonsense vision, that the young readers and poets turned. The Liberation-Generation, as they were called, had either been born in Palestine, now renamed Israel, or had come there at a very young age; to all intents and purposes they were *Tsabres* (natives). They had all participated in the Liberation War, so that their love of the land was of an immediate, first-hand nature. Many of them had lived in *kibutsim.* Neither the excesses of Bialik's verse nor the restraints of the war-years poets (the *Dor Ha-Benayim* or Interim Generation) moved them. Following in the footsteps of the urban poets, Amir Gilbo'a, Shlomo Tan'ee, Khayim Guri, T. Carmi, and Avner Trainin all turned to world literature for their models; only, now the chief sources were English and American literature.

In a country whose political idols rise and fall rapidly, the lease of favorite poets on public adulation is equally brief, and the major urban sophisticates lived long enough to find themselves both criticized and outmoded. In the nineteen fifties and sixties the younger poets, with Natan Zakh as their especially vociferous mouthpiece, began to denounce the artfulness of versification and demanded a prosaic, straightforward language of poetry, a language merely at the service of true feelings and thoughts, rather than an embellishment of these. The younger Hebrew poets, in short, were going the way of William Carlos Williams.

The present decade, however, with the inevitability of oscillating fashions generally, has given rise to different poetic tastes again, and poets like Me'ir Wieseltier and Yonah Wallach are leaning once more in favor of artistry of language and are, with some poetic justice, accusing Natan Zakh and his followers of excessive solipsism. With a return to style and a concern for the world at large, one may imagine oneself back at the beginnings, with Bialik. Yet history does *not* move in circles; the spiral ends never touch, and the present fashion falls somewhere in the spectrum *between* Bialik and Zakh, and far closer to the latter.

And the older poets, by and large, have not sat still. Le'ah Goldberg, in the last years of her life, had demonstrated her ability to make do without the lyricism usually associated with her work, and in the poem "On the Hazards of Smoking" she depicts the heartache and loneliness of old age with wryness and understatement; Amir Gilbo'a, of the Liberation Generation, has taken to experimentation with language. This leveling of the generations has its parallels in world literature; we see in their late work Neruda, W. S. Merwin, and Adrienne Rich, to name a random few, all abandoning strict meter and block-shaped stanzas in favor of the looser forms of the post-Beat generation. And, as with these writers, one finds with the Israeli poets that their early discipline lends a certain backbone to their free verse which the work of the younger poets, lacking their rigorous training, does not always possess.

VIII

A few words should be said, finally, about Hebrew language poetry in the United States. Settlement of the Americas by Jews followed the 1492 expulsion from Spain. In 1642 Isaac da Fonseca Abo'av became the rabbi of the congregation in Pernambuco, Brazil, and set about writing a book of Hebrew poems in the style of the *paytanim;* in it he described his experiences during the war between the Portuguese and Dutch. The first Hebrew poetry book on record in the United States dates back to 1877. Jacob Tsvi Sobel wrote a volume called *Shir Zahav li-Khvod Israel ha-Zaken* (A Golden Song in Honor of the Sage Israel) in which he dealt with the experiences of immigrants.

The group of Hebrew poets which lived and wrote in the United States during the nineteen twenties and thirties has, by and large, now emigrated to Israel, most notably among them are Israel Efrat, Shim'on

Halkin, and T. Carmi. The only well-known figure still writing Hebrew poetry in the United States is Gavri'el Preil. It is a touching gesture, but when one reads his poems about the Maine landscape or the Forty-Second Street Library in New York City, one cannot help but wonder why these American subjects are expressed in a language foreign to them.

The Contemporary Scene

For so short a span (less than a century since Bialik's first poem appeared in print), too great a number of subdivisions into periods and schools exists in modern Hebrew poetry. Seen from an altitude of twenty thousand feet, all parts of the forest merge; only the whole can be distinguished from the wheat fields; from the vantage point of another century or two, it will be the similarities of the present day poetry that will cohere into a picture of the whole.

To gain an understanding of the forest I chose the *analysis* of a single tree from close up, and a *synthesis* of the entire forest, if not from the vantage point of chronological time, at least with the help of geographical distance.

I

Dan Pagis, now in his early fifties, is considered one of the foremost poets writing in Israel today. I found his recent volume, *Brain* (1976), not only stimulating to read but also easy to translate — easier than most of the other poets. I asked myself, why?

Pagis is writing what might be called "international poetry," although its models appear to be mainly English/American. His free verse lines, in the manner of William Carlos Williams, are informal, relaxed. His vocabulary is peppered with foreignisms — *general, elektroni, philodendron, centimeter, sentimentali.* Even the nonpurist is startled by these words nestling amid Biblical language; yet the effect is refreshing — so nothing is sacred after all, one thinks. Translating the poems, consequently, gave me the sense of rendering them back into the language from which they stemmed. Is this kind of internationalization good? Bad? Had one applauded the westernization of Japan? Does one applaud the McDonaldization of Europe? In the global village we share, Pagis's direction seems inevitable.

Pagis frequently employs cinematic shifts — from reality to fantasy, from fact to image, from present to past, from tragedy to comedy, and back again. In "Impromptu Heart" he moves from the reality of the heart to its image, the acrobat. What began as mere metaphor takes on a full-fledged reality of its own: the arena, the horses, the orchestra, all readying for the acrobat's fall. Then, with the last line of the poem, we are deftly returned to the external reality:

But this blue space,
but this free fall,
but this poignant joy, oh Heart.

To the catalog offered in "Fossils" — an archfly trapped in amber, an archconch and archfish in rock — Pagis adds the seemingly incongruous Venus de Milo. From the world of biology we are jolted into the world of art. Yet the archgoddess of love turned marble is not at all out of place among the other abnegators in the poem; we have been prepared for the detail, "whose/arms are air," not only by the reality of the statue's condition, but by the fish who "even renounced itself,/and left only the impress of its bones in the rock." In renouncing her arms Venus has renounced love. The ironic bite of the poem comes from our knowledge that Venus had no more say about the loss of those arms than did the fish about the loss of its body to the molten rock.

In "Point of Origin" we follow the adult speaker meditating "in the library at dusk," through memory, to his childhood. Released from time, he flies rapidly, to the point of motionlessness, into "intergalactic space," leaving behind him "the transparent trail of the past." The science-fiction flight of the rocket into space, again, comes totally unexpectedly yet is precisely right — the past is the fuel which propels the speaker beyond reality, time, and gravity.

In "Two-Legs," reminiscent of Whitman's "Animals" in its cataloguing of human frailties and follies, the list proceeds quite logically when, all at once, the imagination takes off: man is the only creature who "voluntarily rides a motorcycle." Yet this shift to the incongruously comic is immediately reversed with a final irony:

He has twenty fingers,
two ears,
one hundred hearts.

In Pagis's treatment of "objects" one is reminded of Rilke's concern with *die dinge* (things, artifacts). Only, whereas Rilke's poems may conclude on a metaphysical note, those of Pagis stride off into the surrealistic: the armchairs dream of safaris, the souls of the expired balloons hover at nose-level, and the elephant roller-skates on sixteen watches, four to a foot, "right out of his elephantine lot."

Pagis has *not* abandoned his roots. "Brothers" revolves around the fate of Cain, the archmurderer; in "Autobiography" the slain Abel is the speaker who, we learn, has become the archmurdered, Death. Both poems take the Biblical account as their starting point, yet we come away with our perspective widened — Cain is neither quite the criminal nor quite the victim we might have regarded him; and Abel has acquired a patina of horror.

Leaving himself out of his poems like a stage director who knows his business, Pagis allows his cast of subjects to let loose their full imaginative potential. Only in his tone hovers the poet's presence like the smile (or smirk) of the Cheshire cat.

Less so than in some of his more experimental colleagues' work, a sense of *speeding* is nevertheless implicit in Pagis's poetry. As though to compensate for those twenty centuries during which Hebrew literature was reduced to slow motion, the avant-garde Israeli poets appear impatient to explore every new avenue of expression. Ironically, they often arrive at the *deja vu* instead. Gilbo'a's syntactical experiments went out with Gertrude Stein, Avidan's Joycean word play with *Finnegans Wake*. Benjamin Galai's onslaught of foreign expressions, unlike Pagis's more organic use of them, smacks of posturing — *Mon Dieu,* which in Hebrew must be rendered as *Mon Dyu,* simply rings false when the intrinsic *Eli* would have done. On the one hand, it can be argued that Hebrew literature should undergo the experiences of other cultures as soon as and as quickly as possible. On the other hand, I cannot help but wonder whether, like the proverbial turtle, the work of the poet who drags his feet will not ultimately outlive that of the speediest of hares. In the words of Pagis,

> . . . And because he is sentenced to wander, he wanders diligently.
> Exchanges each morning horizon for horizon. One day he discovers:
> The earth has deceived him over the years. It moved, but he, Cain,
> was walking in place.

II

Counteracting the speed element in modern Hebrew poetry is the acute conflict of priorities in the poets' commitments. The *ballon* of Pagis's poetry may derive precisely from his having resolved these conflicts more readily than others. The conflict acts as a force of gravity that pins the poet down and breeds the anguish and doubt which in turn transform into the matter of his poetry.

The conflicts within the Israeli poet may be presented in two triangles, one of an altruistic bent, of duty towards others, and one of a self-centered bent, of duty towards oneself:

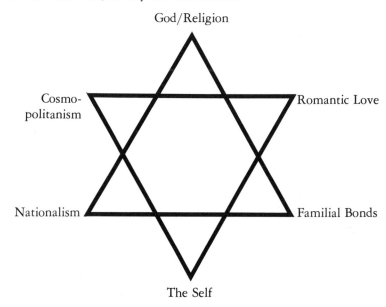

The reader must forgive me if the diagram looks like a bit of Jewish propaganda; the schema just happens to fit, for the tug of loyalties is not in one direction or the other but in several at once.

God/Religion. In the Israeli Jew, religion and nationality are inseparable. The poet Ben-Zion Tomer tells the following anecdote from his Polish childhood:

> When I was four years old, and God only knows how I knew to

distinguish between Yiddish and Hebrew, and in those days in our home they didn't use toilet paper, I remember myself facing a Hebrew newspaper . . . . And no way, no how, was I able to bring myself to use it. . . .

It was neither patriotic loyalty nor religious loyalty but an amalgam of both that had already been instilled in a boy so young. That amalgam is what is usually referred to as Zionism.

In Israel, every child, whether attending parochial or public school, is daily inculcated with his religion. Yet to survive the country must make a separation — pragmatism must be allowed for — the cows fed seven days a week, and traffic kept running. The conflict has been externalized many a time; many a time the orthodox have stoned the buses that violated their Sabbath.

For the poet this common conflict narrows down to arriving at his own religious credo: Is there a God? Is it a personal God? And if so, how is the injustice of the world to be explained? These are of course universal questions, universal doubts; yet because of the tight rein that Jewish religion still holds in Israel even for the iconoclast, it is not easy to arrive at a wholly personal answer. The poet's roots and his concern about the public's reaction to his credo interfere.

It is not surprising then that the scent of prayer should still cling to modern Hebrew poetry. Not only is the language by its very nature still Biblical, but allusions to the Bible, the post-Biblical canon, and prayer books is common. When these allusions dominate the poem, it dies a natural death in the translation; a series of footnotes cannot put it together again.

For examples that do survive we may look at two poems. Eli Netser's "Night Walk," which recounts the pain of loss of a comrade, concludes with the line "And I alone remained to tell." The line can work well enough on its own yet is intensified if we recognize in it the words of the messengers who came to inform Job of his misfortunes; the loss achieves a universal order, the pain is amplified. In Tuvia Rübner's "My Father," the religious paraphernalia (prayer shawl and phylacteries) found in Bialik's poem of the same name are gone; instead, the language derives from the Passover *Hagadah* or prayer book. The first two stanzas begin: "That every night . . . ." and the final stanza, "Tonight . . . ." In the *Hagadah* these phrases initiate the answers to the question "How does this night differ from all other nights?" which the boy traditionally asks of his father on the Passover Eve.

Many recurrent symbols of modern Hebrew poetry still derive simultaneously from the Israeli terrain and the Biblical canon: the sheep, vulture, and dove; the olive, fig, and pomegranate; the mountain, valley, river, and rock.

We live in an age when the extent of our belief in a traditional God is often taken as an inverse measure of our intelligence. The Israeli artist, then, is in double jeopardy — he may be called a naïf, or he will be called a poor Jew. The self must fight against great odds to assert its beliefs unaltered.

Israel Efrat, now in his eighties, writes:

> . . . When God
> lifts the All to His ear
> shall He listen only to the voice of the vast sea,
> or also to me, also to me . . . .

Doubt as to the efficacy of communication is here, but not a doubt as to the existence of God.

The gap widens with some of the younger poets. Natan Zakh, a contemporary of Pagis, compares God to a man sitting at the edge of the street, watching passersby who are oblivious to his presence.

The speaker in Dov Khomsky's "The Distance from Me to You" is more bitterly outspoken, complaining of the inequalities between himself and God; yet the very complaint betrays belief, just as did the older poets'. When Bialik, in "On the Slaughter," cries out,

> Ah, Heavens, intercede for me!
> If a god in you there be, and he hold concourse among you —
> (He has eluded me)
> Then you must pray for me!

it is the fervent belief in God, outraged by the injustice of the pogroms, which prompts the outcry. If the speaker truly believed there was no God, he could not have expected universal justice.

In a country where death through violence is a daily occurrence, the survivors must grapple with the belief in the soul and its immortality. To Benjamin Galai the answer is clear and brutal, right out of Ecclesiastes:

And the soul of man? Does it live forever?
Who'll promise us — a charity or curse?
Rather a living dog than a dead lion,
For life is never proffered twice.

Again, Dan Pagis can make fun of the souls of balloons suspended in
limbo, but to Israel Efrat and many other poets the soul is still very real
and sacrosanct.

The Israeli poets have been criticized for not devoting enough of their
writings to the holocaust. Possibly the horror of that experience is even
today still liable to overwhelm the poets' art, and so, wisely, they shy
away. In the poems that have dealt with the holocaust great control and
indirection have been exercised. In Pagis's "Autobiography" the
speaker, Death, does not wish to "weary" us with the tale. In Ya'akov
Beser's "In the Beginning My Mother Screeched" the unidentified
marauders arrive in the very last stanza upon the scene of a demolished
kindergarten:

Quickly
they came through the garden beds
ashes
smoke-grey lizards
planted their tails in the sky.

Hardly a breath is taken between "their" arrival and the ashes — cause
strikes like lightning, produces effect. The image of the lizards
combines retroactively with the mother's screech at the poem's
beginning to evoke the terror which it took Bialik pages to create when
writing of the Russian pogroms in "In the City of Slaughter."

Itamar Ya'oz-Kest's *Ordeal by Fire* does tackle the Bergen-Belsen
experience directly. Yet even here the outcry is muted, and "the head of
a beast sprouted on the neck" in the deportation train could refer equally
to the inhuman guards and the dehumanized victims.

Nationalism. The poet is caught between the pressures, both external
and internal, to further the cause of his country and uphold its traditions
on the one hand, and on the other to express his own artistic truth in a
cosmopolitan framework. He knows that only the latter direction can
assure his work's qualification as art and its survival in time. The short
life span of patriotic and topical poetry can be seen in the work of the
Kibuts poets of the early twentieth century; it has simply not held up.

Even mere optimism has a way of wearing thin quickly, as poems like Amir Gilbo'a's "Against the Wind" and Avner Trainin's "Sunbeams" demonstrate. Even social criticism, which it takes courage to write in a country struggling for survival, comes over as merely reverse propaganda, and Mosheh Dor's "Safety Pin" is saved only by its satirical bite.

In the manner of the medieval Spanish poets, many a poem is written to celebrate the Israeli cities, Jerusalem in particular. These poems, even when critical, are imbued with deep love and contrast sharply with poems written about foreign locales. Le'ah Goldberg in *The Italian Poems* exercises her mordant wit much more freely than she does when writing about the Tel Aviv of the thirties. And Daliah Rabikovich's "How Hong Kong Was Destroyed" swings readily into surrealism. Perhaps in writing about foreign places the artist is freed from the internal censorship of his national loyalties.

Again criticism has been leveled at the poets for not dealing with the Israeli-Arab conflict. And again, as in the case of the holocaust, the poets are most likely, intuitively, doing the only thing possible — maintaining their silence. If they were to propagandize for Israel they would prostitute their art; and to write freely, even think freely, public pressure, or the expectations of such pressure, would render impossible.

Nevertheless, the poets who fought in the Liberation War are beginning to speak out; they do not name specific events, times, places, yet their sentiments are clear. In the poem beginning

The diameter of the bomb was thirty centimeters
and the diameter of its hitting-range about seven meters
and within it four dead and eleven wounded. . . .

Yehudah Amikhai comes close to lecturing, but in "My Father" he speaks poignantly of the parent's futile efforts to protect his son from war. And Benjamin Galai does not spare his readers' feelings:

Their names interred in darkness now — Lord God of Hosts!
One by one set out, did not arrive.
Slain the adolescent returns unto his dust
And through his mouth a profusion of roots drives.

Death here is a cold fact, and time is yet another:

Since not forever shall your sweetheart mourn you

And not forever look demurely down.
In your native village — the bells are tolling
As though you'd never left, and did not return.

Familial Ties. Conflicts arising from parental and marital relationships are of course not peculiarly Israeli, yet the closeness of Jewish familial ties exacerbate them.

Three of the poems in this volume are titled "My Father," and many more deal with the father-son relationship; for in Hebrew literature it, rather than the Oedipal mother-son relation, is dominant. The guilt and recriminations often found in these poems point either way: the speaker feels he has failed the father, usually the *dead* father, has not loved him enough, supported him enough, *or* he feels that the father had not loved *him* enough, had failed him in his expectations:

> — Where is the path, Father, leading home?
> — My Son, the path leading home, is where?
> — I'm afraid, Father, it's getting dark!
> — My Son, it's getting dark and I'm afraid! . . .

writes Itamar Ya'oz-Kest in the poem-sequence *My Father — Is the Root.* The father from whom guidance is sought is here a mere echo of his son, the same impotence and terror afflict both, and the poet comes away with an admixture of pity and reproach. In "At a Loss" Mosheh Dor takes up the same theme from the vantage point of the father and comes away full of self-recriminations and compassion:

> I go on smiling (my Lord, Naked I stand before You
> and vast is the night all about)
> and bend over my son:
> "Look, a bird! Look, a cat!"

Focus on the father-son relationship accounts for the virtually dozens of poems interpreting the would-be sacrifice of Isaac by his father Abraham. Benjamin Galai, however, looks at the Biblical account from the point of view of Sarah, the mother:

> . . . the coffin in which she lay had been made all those years
> out of the memory of split logs on another mountain,
> on another mountain, in the Land of Moriah.

The poet does not explain the exact nature of Sarah's grief; we can only surmise that her husband's betrayal of herself and her son, prevented only by God's miraculous intervention, had killed her spirit long before the death of her body.

Poems treating with marriage are rare; perhaps Rilke's dictum that the unfulfilled loves are so much greater than the consummated ones has something to do with it. And the marriage relationship, even when tackled, may remain unspecified. In Alterman's "Tonight" the couple that has known each other for a long time and shares one bed has all the earmarks of marriage, but we are not told.

Romantic Love. Poems about unrequited love and love gone sour are as common in Hebrew as elsewhere. The conflicts here are not with traditional marriage and religion; the bulk of the conflict occurs instead between expectations and reality. Sara Teasdale's lines come to mind: "The heart asks more than life can give." In the love poems of Esther Raab and, to a lesser extent, in those of Le'ah Goldberg, there is a disturbing sense of self-abnegation in the face of the male lover; a sense of a Prince Charming and a Cinderella who never quite came out from behind her stove. And yet, even as these women seem to put their entire lives on the line of love, we must remember that artists by their very calling are voracious exploiters of experience who garner from their agony the honey of their future songs.

We find in many a poem, too, the sense of inadequacy of the male lover; the speaker in T. Carmi's "Waking" dreads having to face his beloved in the light of day. And in Natan Zakh's "It Becomes from Year to Year" the inadequate male is annihilated by the female's shallow ego-boosting techniques.

Although outnumbered, there are also poems of love fulfilled; these tend to be joyously and matter-of-factly heterosexual. Aharon Amir's love poems charm with their innocence and yearning; yet with the absence of guilt and conflict comes a diminution of power.

Friendship. Between familial and romantic ties, friendship (not shown in the schema) nestles comfortably. The admiration of one male for another satisfies some of the need for paternal affection, while the loyalty is imbued with some of the mystique of a love affair. Yet here, too, conflicts arise; for many of the friendship poems are elegies, and personal loss is poised against national necessity. In Ori Bernstein's "Conversations" we find self-recriminations for surviving the friend:

You go through the motions of the dead.
It's new to you. You do not fit.

Now you ask and no one answers.
A view of the earth is your share.
And the days I count already
exceed your days. And are fair.

Cosmopolitanism. Discussing the subject of international ambitions in an interview, the late poet Yekhi'el Mar said:

> If you are a writer in your own nation, it means a great deal. And if they love you in your own nation, if they love your poetic essence, and every writer wants that they should love him . . . that they should hear what he has to say. . . . I don't care whether they hear me in Denmark. I want to be heard in Tel Aviv, in Ramat-Gan and in Jerusalem. What will happen later, doesn't count. It will happen — sure, everyone dreams, or doesn't dream, it doesn't matter. Certainly Agnon [the novelist] at the end also wanted to win the Nobel Prize, but first he penned his Jews.

Both criticism and guilt may follow when a writer turns from traditional Hebrew culture to cosmopolitanism. Nevertheless, the modes of European and American poetry have been absorbed and emulated by the Hebrew poets, and the mythology of other cultures been drawn on. Efrat's Narcissus, Tomer's Don Quixote, and Guri's Odysseus-cum-Rip-Van-Winkle all serve as appropriate symbols for the poets' conflicts.

The Self. Weighed down, pulled and tugged at by so many opposing forces, the self is coerced into song. In the words of Israel Efrat:

They say the bird sings
more sweetly
when blinded.

In the end the true artist seeks more than anything to remain faithful to his own vision; and if in the process he betrays causes, why then, to paraphrase Whitman, he betrays them.

III

Because, as the selection in this volume illustrates, Hebrew women poets are far outnumbered by the men, a separate, brief evaluation of them is called for. With the exception of Le'ah Goldberg, who died in 1970, none of the women have achieved stellar fame. From the pioneering days only Rachel is still remembered, if not read. Yokheved Bat-Miriam is admired chiefly for her *Ghetto Poems,* and Esther Raab and Miriam Yalan Shteklis are still holding the traditional fort.

Zelda (born 1914) demonstrates a fine feel for language; the whole, larger than the sum of its parts, shines. Of an old woman she writes:

Her thin flesh has evaporated
and gleams in the dark like an ancient tale —
stirring revulsion in corpulent men
and in the green leaves of the mulberry.

Tsfrirah Gar (born in 1924) writes along a similar frequency; her poems tend to be lucid and genuine.

Best known and most admired of the younger women poets is Daliah Rabikovich (born in 1936). Her style is often banal and dissonant — a deliberate device which echoes the voices of the victimized women in her poems: the woman as mechanical doll or sex object; the woman as a modern Creusa wearing the flaming gown of her gender; the woman reduced to imbecility, having only one readily pacified craving — "Give her vanilla."

Why the disproportion between men and women poets? One hesitates to speculate. Perhaps another conflict is at bottom, and despite the seeming equality of women (who serve in the Israeli army and work the land) the system of society is still, in the Biblical tradition, essentially patriarchal.

The Hebrew Language

Entering the burial chamber of an ancient king must be something like it; that thrill of examining a segment of the *Torah* or leafing through the pages of a Hebrew Bible. One feels in the presence of a work, some of it over three thousand years old, preserved intact in its contents, and identical yet in its language — its diction, its script, and its pronunciation. Incredible, and altogether false.

The older books of the Bible were reworked by later editors so that neither content nor language is quite the same. The script of the original was the ancient alphabet which was gradually abandoned in favor of the present "square script" around the beginning of the Christian era. And because the writing was devoid of vowel-points, we cannot tell how the Hebrew of those days was pronounced; the vowel-points added around the ninth century merely reflect the pronunciation of that period. And as to general appearance, the original left no spaces between words; roughly, it looked like this:

INTHBGNNGGDCRTDTHHVNSANDTH
EARTHTHEARTHWSWTHOUTFRMAND
VDANDDRKNSSWSUPNTHFCEOFTHDP

A shrewd guess and a little effort will identify this as the opening of the Book of Genesis; yet who today would want to read a chapter, let alone a book, that poses such difficulties?

Even if the thrill is somewhat dampened, the magic of the Bible and the miracle of its preservation are still overwhelming. And while the older *prose* may not have come down to us, scholars believe that the *poetry* was transmitted intact. The language of the Song of Deborah, for example, is in the Northern dialect of Israel, which, as the isolationism of the two states abated, was replaced by an amalgam of Northern and Southern (or Judean) dialects. And although one cannot say for sure how that dialect was pronounced, the vocabulary of that three-thousand-year-old poem is still part of today's Hebrew.

Other languages have, like Latin, petrified, or else shed their skin periodically. Thus, Anglo-Saxon gave way to Middle English, which in turn made way for modern English. With each change-over a large portion of the earlier stage was jettisoned. Hebrew, on the other hand, has, with a curious avarice, accumulated its layers of language like tree rings, and diction thousands of years apart functions comfortably today within a single sentence: *Ishto tilfena* is perfectly idiomatic modern Hebrew: *ishto* (his wife) derives from the noun *isha,* first found in the second chapter of the Book of Genesis; *tilfena* (telephoned) is, of course, a recently imported foreignism.

Not only the vocabulary but the idiom of the Bible is still viable, and while we can hardly say in English, "Thou findest favor in my eyes," the Biblical phrase is part of the modern and pragmatic Israeli's conversation: *Atah motseh* (or, *at motset,* in the feminine) *khen be'enay.*

Hebrew is a Semitic language. Coming from the Babylonian north, the Tribes of Israel may have originally spoken a form of Akkadian (i.e., Babylonian or Aramaic). In the Land of Canaan they were steeped in the languages of their neighbors: the Canaanite (or Phoenician), the Amoritic, Moabite, Ugaritic, and the non-Semitic Hittite; the Egyptian sojourn, too, left its mark on the language. Hebrew, consequently, has been considered a *lashon me'urbelet*, or mixed language.

The ancient Hebrew script clearly derives from pictographs or ideographs. The names of many of the letters today still echo what the ancient script had depicted visually. The first letter, *Alef*, or ox, was written in the shape of an ox's head, and today's symbol still retains the animal's horns. *Gimel*, meaning camel, was represented by a hump; *dalet*, or door, by a triangle — the entrance-way of a tent; *vav*, or nail, was written just so; *mem*, water, was a series of waves; and *ayin*, eye, looked like one.

It is this Hebraic-Phoenician alphabet that the Greeks took over and, by converting some of the expendable letters into vowels, adapted to their own linguistic needs. Greek could no more be deciphered without vowels than English can, yet the nature of Hebrew is such that the vowel-points are, to this day, expendable. Its vocabulary is derived from three-letter clusters whose meaning, as they undergo various declensions and conjugations, remains fixed:

MaHeR	quickly
leMaHeR	to hurry
MeHiRut	speed (n.)

Each English word here has a different root; in the Hebrew M-H-R is common to all three words. A newcomer to Hebrew, therefore, need only come to recognize the basic clusters to be able to understand some words he had never encountered before.

Again:

GaDoL	big, large, great, adult
liGDoL	to grow
leGaDeL	to raise, educate, glorify
lehitGaDeL	to boast
lehaGDiL	to increase
GiDuL	growth, tumor
GaDLut	magnitude
GoDeL	size
miGDaL	tower, tall structure

In so-called weak forms one of the letters disappears in certain conjugations, and some clusters have *four* letters; these latter are often a two-letter cluster repeated for onomatopoetic effect:

leGaMGeM	to stammer
lePaRPeR	to twitch
leRaFReF	to flutter
lePaTPeT	to chatter

The three-letter-root theory was not formulated till the medieval Spanish period, and it is now being disputed. Today's linguists argue that Hebrew may originally have been based on a *two*-letter root-cluster, and evidence to that effect is considerable. Many Hebrew clusters, especially those depicting action or motion, share two of their root letters and vary only in the third. As civilization became more complex, certain general verbs may have required refinement, and their two-letter roots were given a number of third letters to distinguish them:

NaKaV	to perforate, pierce
NaKaD	to point, prick
NaKaT	to seize, take
NaKaH	to sprain
NaKaR	to pierce, pick at, pluck out
NaKaSH	to strike, knock

The letters N and K are common to all these verbs, and all the actions are refinements of one general one.

Ambiguity is rare. When a single three-letter cluster has more than one meaning, it is because an earlier distinct sound has atrophied, and the letter that had originally designated it merged with one still extant; two different words, consequently, are now pronounced and written alike.

Ambiguity may at times occur where words which share the same root appear to be identical yet belong to different parts of speech, as in these lines from a poem by Abba Kovner: *Vehoo amar lah: r'ee/r'ee,* which can be translated as, "And he said to her: A mirror, a mirror," or as, "And he said to her: Look! Look!" or as a fusion of the two, "Look, a mirror," or "A mirror, look." The imperative feminine, second-person singular of "to look" and the masculine-singular noun from the same root, meaning "mirror," are both *r'ee* in the Hebrew. This particular ambiguity is never resolved in the poem, yet in a prose context we would soon find out whether a mirror was about and whether a woman was addressed.

The absence of vowel-points in most of today's prose does lead to a degree of ambiguity: *h-z-k-n-h   k-f-ts-h   a-l-v* is what we may read in a magazine article. The roots of the first two words are readily recognizable — *z-k-n*, to age, and *k-f-ts*, to jump; the first word is a feminine noun with an article as prefix; the second word is a feminine, third-person-singular verb in the past tense; the last word is a preposition declined in the third person, masculine, singular. That much is plain; yet the phrase could be read either as

hazkenah kaftsa alav, "the old lady jumped on him," or
haziknah kaftsa alav, "old age jumped on him," or "old age overcame
                him" (a perfectly natural Hebrew idiom)

In context, however, the confusion would at worst be temporary and good for a laugh.

Ambiguity, on the other hand, would run rampant in English if the vowels were omitted: b-t, for example, could be read as:

bat	bite
bait	boot
bet	boat
beet	but
beat	butt
bit	butte

Many of these words have no relationship whatever to each other; the poor reader would merely flounder.

By the ninth century C.E. the absence of vowels became a source of difficulty even in the Hebrew. As the language became progressively literary rather than spoken, doubt and insecurity along with a compulsion to be precise led to the adoption of the Arabic system of vowel-points. The Babylonian and Palestinian variations placed the vowel-points above the words; the Tiberian, which ultimately won out, placed them underneath. Much resistance had to be overcome for the vowel-points to be introduced into the *Torah*. The conservatives held that the word of God was not to be tampered with; the progressives countered that while God had written the Ten Commandments, the rest of the Old Testament was written by man. In the end pragmatism won out.

Pragmatism may also account for the ready adoption into Hebrew of some of the vocabulary of those cultures with which the Jews came into close contact. During the Babylonian, Persian, Greek, and Roman empires, the language of the conquerors left its impress on Hebrew in varying degrees. Thus, during the Mishnaic period of the first and second century C.E., one finds many Aramaic words in the language: *Sinar* (apron), *gar'in* (grain), *agas* (pear), *sharvool* (sleeve), *niyar* (paper). The tendency may have been to use the Aramaic words secularly and the Biblical ones religiously. Thus, we read in the Mishna a ruling as to which blessing should be said upon eating fruit:

Al perot ha-ilan omer: 'boreh pri ha-ets.'
For the fruit of the *tree* he will say: 'The bringer-forth of the fruit of the *tree.*'

The instruction uses the Aramaic form of the word *tree, ilan,* yet the blessing itself retains the Biblical form, *ets.*

The Greek terms that had entered the language by the Mishnaic period include *te'atron* (theatre), *ambatia* (bath), *hediot* (idiot, in the sense of "common fellow"), *avir* (air, ether). The Roman terms referred largely to military, architectural, and governmental functions (*ligyon,* legion, e.g.).

In the centuries that followed, Arabic, Turkish, Spanish, French, Italian, German, Russian, and Polish all contributed some of their vocabulary to the Hebrew. And conversely, as the Jews adopted the language of a particular country, they imbued it with their Hebrew usages and wrote it in their Hebrew script. Yiddish, which is a dialect of the German, not only developed its own literature but turned around and bequeathed *its* idiom back to the Hebrew. Ladino, similarly, was a dialect of the Spanish, written in Hebrew script, and French, Italian, Arabic, Turkish, and some Slavic languages each had their own Jewish dialect.

During the *Haskalah* period Hebrew received much of its new lifeblood from the *Khasidic* folk-Hebrew. The *Khasidic* (or Devout) movement had sprung up in the middle of the eighteenth century in Poland and instilled religious worship with a sense of exuberance and brotherhood. Similar folk elements, although of a secular kind, influenced Hebrew during the days of the *Aliyot,* the early migrations to

1 Introduction

Palestine, when the *po'alim,* or workers, adapted the Hebrew to their daily needs.

During that latter period the Sephardic of the Arabic and Spanish Jews was chosen as the offical Palestinian Hebrew rather than the Ashkenazy of Central and Eastern Europe. The accent on the majority of words, consequently, fell on the ultimate syllable whereas in the Ashkenazy it fell on the *pen*ultimate one. The undotted *taf* was pronounced as a *t* rather than as a sibilant, and the pronunciation of several vowels was also affected. Yet marked variations existed even *within* the Sephardic and the Ashkenazy dialects, and there can be no question as to which of these is the "correct" one.

The origin of the two dialects is disputed; the Sephardic may have come to Spain from the Land of Israel via Babylon; the Ashkenazy may have been the Palestinian dialect around the ninth century C.E.

Today Hebrew is growing rapidly. Scientific and technological progress require new words. Some of these are simply imported (*telefon, telegraf, televisya*); others are wrought from established roots. At times several words surface for a single object: *Kali'ah* and *til* both meant "missile," but the former term was eventually abandoned. *Mani'ah* and *mano'ah* both meant "motor"; only *mano'ah* survived. Such weeding out is not to be taken for granted, however. *Tsalmaniyah, tsalmoniyah,* and *matslemah,* all denoting a camera, continue in use simultaneously.

The effect of mass communication and cross-culturization, too, requires a constant broadening of the Hebrew vocabulary: *Vodka, vermoot,* and *veeskee, kontsert* and *kenggeroo* and *planetah* are just a smattering of the international potpourri that has become part of the language today.

Conceivably, now that Hebrew is proliferating and modernizing so extensively, it may have to begin to slough off some of its older skins and perhaps yield up some of its Biblical treasures. Particular concern is voiced about the "Anglo-Saxon invasion." Yet such an invasion is hardly to be wondered at when English is Israel's second language and its passport to the world at large. The poet Ben-Zion Tomer, asked whether he thought Hebrew was threatened by the foreign influences, commented that there was no point in boasting of one's linguistic impoverishment and that "the encounter with the culture of a foreign tongue is not dangerous as long as one's roots are deep. In such instances, one's own language wins out." And, as we have seen, the roots of the Hebrew run deep.

Hebrew Poetics

Much like the Jews themselves, Hebrew poetics endured a long journey from Biblical times to the present; and just as the language of a country where Jews had settled would affect their Hebrew, so, too, that country's poetic modes: Arab, Italian, German and Russian, French and finally English and American poetry have effected great changes in Hebrew poetry as first encountered in the Bible.

Pressed to define what poetry is, one may usually begin with: "Language broken up into lines . . . ." This visual concept of poetry, and usually its lowest common denominator, while applicable to modern Hebrew poetry will not serve to define Biblical poetry — as a look at any psalm will show. One is tempted to speculate how some of our own modern-day free verse would hold up if written out in paragraphs; would it retain its poetic identity? And how does Biblical verse still bear the distinct impress of poetry?

Our own poetry, and later Hebrew poetry as well, is a continuous construct that gathers internal tension through the line breaks. The opposition, especially between line endings and a sense and grammar still in midstream, gives the poem momentum. Biblical poetry, quite to the contrary, consists of a series of "individually wrapped" units or verses in which the grammatical finish coincides with the end of the verse. The closed classical couplets of Pope, for example, would be a reasonable facsimile, but *without the rhyme and the meter.*

Each verse of Biblical poetry consists of a cluster of two or three (rarely more) weights which balance each other much like the baubles on a Calder mobile. We can start out with *any* phrase:

> It is raining

then add to it another of similar weight:

> It is raining it is cold

or yet another:

> It is raining it is cold it is winter.

Instead of short and equal weights, we could add a heavier phrase and let it balance the lighter one the way two objects of disparate size balance each other in a modern painting:

It is raining the moon is behind the clouds.

The verse following would probably be a similar construct:

It is raining the moon is behind the clouds
No star in sight darkness has covered the land.

How exactly do we measure these "weights"? Intuitively, it is as easy as weighing pebbles in the palms of our hands; we *feel* it. Scientifically, attempts have recently been made to measure the verses by counting the stresses and feeding them into a computer for an overall profile. The resulting patterns are so complex as to hardly deserve to be called patterns; to a poet or reader they would be of no help whatever. And yet the weights and the pull they exercise on each other are as real as gravity.

Some of this effect of balance is clearly achieved through a reliance on repetition:

repetition of grammatical form, or parallelism
repetition of diction
reiteration of ideas, and
negative reiteration of ideas, or antithesis.

Shakespeare's old saw, "To be or not to be," could pass for a perfect Biblical verse. It has balance between a lighter and a heavier weight; the two parts are grammatically parallel, the diction is repeated, and the idea is reiterated through antithesis. We have not strayed far from Ecclesiastes:

A time to plant and a time to rip out the planted
A time to kill and a time to heal
A time to shatter and a time to build
A time to weep and a time to laugh
A time to mourn and a time to dance . . .

Something chant-like, ritualistic, builds through the use of repetition.

A denominator which Biblical poetry *does* share with present-day poetry is the ubiquitous use of imagery. "They were lighter than eagles, they were stronger than lions," illustrates the use of simile. And the extended metaphor of the shepherd and his crook leading his flock by the still waters of the Twenty-third Psalm, reminiscent of some of Homer's elaborate comparisons, needs hardly to be quoted.

Rhyme (*and* assonance, or inexact rhyme) occurs only rarely and accidentally in the Bible; it does not become a conscious device until the time of the *Paytanim*, of whom Yosi Ben Yosi was the first to indulge. However, the other predominant device of the *Paytanim*, the acrostic, does derive from the Bible (Psalms 119 and 145; Proverbs 31, Echa 3). Each verse of the acrostic Biblical chapter begins with a letter of the alphabet, from *Alef* through *Taf* (i.e., *A* through *Z*). The device offers few of the rewards that a modern acrostic might reap from the hurdles which the imagination must overcome to begin each line with the proper letter. In Biblical poetry each verse is, after all, a new sentence; any letter could be employed quite easily; and Hebrew does not even have the *x* and *z* for the poet to tangle with.

The postcanonical *Paytanim*, or writers of prayer-poems, used the acrostic both forwards and backwards (i.e., from *Z* to *A*), used it to sign their own names and others', and found esoteric ways to hide their acrostics, putting them, for example, as the second rather than the first letter of each line, and then omitting lines in between. Yet, besides the heavy use of acrostics and of rhyme, the poetry remained essentially Biblical.

The first major changes in Hebrew poetry came through the innovations of Dunash Ben Labrat (ca. 920–ca.990). Since he was born in Baghdad and reared in North Africa, Arabic poetry was part of his heritage, and when he moved to live in Spanish Cordova he began to advocate in his writings the adoption of Arabic meters in Hebrew poetry.

The poets of the golden age of Spain *all* wrote in the Arab meters, and because of their vast influence on Jewish communities elsewhere, the Hebrew poets of Italy, Provence, Germany, France, and England adopted the Arab meters and continued to write in them for centuries. Even Yemenite Jews in Saudi Arabia adopted the meters originating in their own culture only by the circuitous way of Spain.

As in Greek and Latin qualitative verse, the Arabic relies on the alternation of long and short syllables. The syllables considered long contained the vowels, whereas those considered short contained the *shva* — designating either a nonsound or a colorless, neutral sound to which any of the vowels may at times disintegrate. The most common of the metrical patterns possible (some reckon sixteen in Arabic, eighteen in Hebrew) are:

$$-\cup- \quad \cup-- \quad \cup--- \quad -\cup-- \quad --\cup-$$

where $\cup$ designates a short, and $-$ a long syllable. Unlike the Arabic, and because of differing rules regarding the use of the *shva*, Hebrew uses a large number of spondees, a pattern of two long syllables per foot (- -):

ktōnēt /pāsīm /lāvāsh /hā-gān/ ūksūt /rīkmāh /midēy /dīsh'ō/

The line of poetry, called *bayit*, was, like the English alliterative verse line, divided in half with the two parts called "ribs" (*tsla'ot*). The first rib was the "door" or opener; the second rib was the closing.

Along with the Arabic meters came the Arabic forms. Long poems were constructed around a single rhyme, with all the closings rhyming (but not the "doors"). Think of an English poem in which sixty-five lines rhyme with "sheep"! Hebrew is rhyme-rich enough to make it possible, although at times even the great Yehudah Ha-Levi had to stoop to forcing.

Precisely because Hebrew is easily rhymed, poets created certain deliberate obstacles for themselves; for what is a game without challenges? Thus, a strong rhyme was preferred to a weak one; and the perfectly legitimate English rhymes *retúrn-concérn* or *contradíction-depíction* would be considered weak rhymes in Hebrew because the rules call for the repetition of the beginning consonants of the last stressed syllables: con*cern*-dis*cern* or contra*dict*ion-ad*dict*ion, rhymes which would be frowned upon in English as being identical. Poets also looked down on rhymes which were based entirely on grammatical inflection rather than on part of the stem of the word: *salkhá* (your basket) and *harkhá* (your mountain) look like strong rhymes, yet the stressed syllables are merely the inflections for the possessive case, second person, masculine, singular. *Harkhá* and *karkhá* (your pillow) on the other hand would be acceptable because the *r* of the main stems, *har* and *kar*, is shared.

A popular form adopted from the Arabic was the *meroobah*, or square poem. The first three "ribs" of each two-line stanza of the *meroobah* rhyme with each other, and the fourth "ribs" of all the stanzas rhyme in turn, as in this short poem by Yehudah Ha-Levi:

The waves would hum	like wheels on the run
and clouds lightly come	across the sea's scroll.

Dark now its skies	its waters tyrannize
its lower depths rise	and take their toll.

The first break away from the Arabic qualitative verse was made by Mosheh of Rieti (1398–1460), who felt that the technique was alien to the Biblical tradition. He turned instead to the syllabic verse of his own Italian culture. Syllabic verse was taken up by some of the poets of Sefed in Palestine, yet a significant shift to syllabic verse did not occur until the arrival of the *Haskalah*. The well-known *Songs of Glory (Shirey Tif'eret)* by Naftali Herts Wessely (1725–1805) are a case in point. First considered alexandrines in the French manner, with a thirteenth syllable added by the feminine endings, the lines are now regarded as a variation on the Italian hendecasyllabics (eleven syllable lines). The thirteen syllable variation had been used previously in Latin poetry, and today one American poet regards himself as the discoverer of the form in English.

The next transformation of Hebrew poetics came with Mordekhai Mannë (1859–86), who first introduced the accentual-syllabic verse of traditional English poetry into Hebrew verse; Mannë and his contemporaries borrowed the meter from German and Russian poetry.

Accentual-syllabic verse depends on the alternation of stressed and unstressed syllables in a line, and here a problem arose: should the accent fall on the ultimate syllable of words in the Sephardic way, or on the *pen*ultimate syllable in the manner of the Ashkenazy? One or the other form had to be settled on before a coherent meter could evolve. The choice fell on the Ashkenazy.

The stress patterns are identical to the English — iamb, trochee, anapest, dactyl, spondee, and the less familiar amphibrach. Khayim Nakhman Bialik, writing accentual-syllabic verse in the Ashkenazy, was simply following in the tradition established some years before. In "After My Death," he begins:

Ākhrĕy̆/mōtī/sīpdŏŏ/kăkhă lī
After/dying/mourn you/thus for me

a pattern of three trochees and a final dactyl which he sustains throughout the poem.

Yet reading the poem today, in the Sephardic, the meter is violated:

Ắkhreȳ/mŏtī/sĭpdōō/kặkhắ lĭ

The trochees all turn into iambs and only the final dactyl remains intact.

The changes which Hebrew poetics have undergone in this century parallel those of our global village at large. German Expressionism, French Symbolism, Imagism, and the "Impure Poetry" advocated by Neruda and William Carlos Williams have all been avidly assimilated into Hebrew verse by poets with cosmopolitan aspirations. A certain irony lies in the instance of poets emulating someone like Walt Whitman, who was himself so heavily influenced by the Bible — here the Hebrew poet has come full circle via a very circuitous route and, like the serpent, is devouring his own tail.

ON THE HAZARDS OF TRANSLATION

Moses descending from Mount Sinai did not know, we are told (Exodus 34:29), *ki karan or panav* — which may mean either "that his face *shone*" or "that it *had sprouted horns.*" At least one translator had made a silly choice, and Michelangelo immortalized his mistake.

Not all translation errors are that blatant, yet ambiguity of language is behind many of them. In Me'ir Wieseltier's poem "+30°C," the word *makoshim* occurs. It can mean "piano keys" or "shovels." Wooed by the context of snow and the north, I opted for:

snow falls
on the shovels
the deer of the north
wag their heads.

Piano keys were definitely out. Only when the meaning of the poem, the identity of the "contraption" as the poet's *typewriter* suggested itself did the third and proper choice come to me:

snow falls
across the keys.

For it is the typewriter which is snowed in, the absence of poetic inspiration that turns a +30°C day into a North Pole experience.

One must always make choices. The last line in a poem by Le'ah Goldberg reads, "*Ve'atah zmani veshiri.*" Since *shir* can mean either "poem" or "song," a literal translation would be: "And you are my time and my poem/song." I readily chose "song" over "poem" yet felt that "you are my time," while fine in Hebrew, was not idiomatic in English. I chose "And you — my clock and my song." Did I have the right to introduce "clock"?

The answer would depend on what one expected from a translation. If it is to be a word for word transcription of the original, "clock" has no place in the line. If, on the other hand, one preferred a gestalt rendition, a seamless whole that lives and breathes as a poem in its new garments, then such liberties are inevitable; although the work must never stray from the original, must never become the translator's showpiece.

Perhaps the only way to avoid all the hazards is not to translate at all. The next safest way is to pick only those poems which are readily translatable. To the use of this subterfuge I must plead guilty. When I did not understand a poem as a totality or failed to work through a particular line, phrase, or even word, or found the ambiguities too unwieldy, I put the poem aside. I have always marveled at the courage, or foolhardiness, of the translators of Mallarmé's work; now I wonder too at the *khuzpah* of the translators of David Avidan's *Impossible Poems*.

I selected those poems which moved me or touched me in some way. If I felt a poem was inferior or just did not work in the original, I could not see improving on it to make it work in the English. Sometimes, too, the poem did work, did move me in the Hebrew, yet died in transit and had to be shelved. The notion, therefore, of translating a poet's entire oeuvre is staggering. How does one get around the recalcitrant pieces?

So much for the negative aspects of selecting the poems. The joy of discovering those poems that yes, yes, I could refashion in another language is like discovering a thimble-sized Pacific day after day. And the joy of the translating process itself is almost as great as writing one's own poems. In some ways it is greater: one does not have to undergo the terror of creating out of nothing — the proven blueprint is already there; nor does one have to feel responsible for the quality of the work itself. No wonder some people like painting by numbers.

Evenings, in my reclining chair, dictionary to one side, anthologies to the other, I would scribble out half a dozen translations. Later, or the next morning, at the typewriter, there would be changes — and always at the typewriter, with the hard work already done, the ear suddenly would discover a better rhythm, the unconscious would provide a more organic phrase.

Although I did not set down any rules for myself, I adhered to many intuitively. The priorities, those sacred cows which were under no circumstances to be sacrificed (in a process which cannot occur without sacrifices), were sense and rhythm. Not only was the sense of the whole to be transferred intact, but the sense of the particulars as well. No changes were to be admitted to accommodate the rhyme, nor any extraneous words added to pad out the lines for a certain meter. At the same time, the rhythm of the lines was to be preserved. A tall order.

Yet I had few qualms about other sacrifices. While retaining rhyme in translation, I felt free to substitute inexact rhymes for exact ones and vice versa. And I let the rhyme schemes determine themselves in the English, as I felt they must have determined themselves for the poets in

Hebrew. Thus, if the original used a scheme of *aabb,* but the English tended more easily to rhyme *abab,* I let it. Surprisingly, as in the final stanza of Alterman's "Summer Night," an occasional superfluity of riches occurred, and an *abba* or *abab* stanza would be rhymed *aaaa,* with just a single rhyme, in other words, instead of the two of the original.

The rhyme, however, was not to be forced nor the syntax inverted to achieve that rhyme. Nor would I admit antiquated language (a single "alas" in a poem by Bialik escaped me; I could find no substitute).

To illustrate the differences, and similarities, of English and Hebrew prosody and syntax, here is a *literal* translation of Yekhi'el Mar's poem "One Tiny Bird."

BIRD SMALL ONE

all his-life he-sought bird one small
that-would-stand to-his-right
on his-right or on his-left.
all his-life he-sought to discover understanding
with the-sons-of his-kind
but not he-changed his-voice
to lure that-same bird singing
to his-nest
to his-all
that she-would-stand her thus on his-right
or on his-left
and-would-sing on-his-behalf
without to-fear and-without
to-be his.

only that-she-would-stand her thus without intent
to-understand-him
and-without to-stray from-her-business.
and-her-voice in-his-voice
and-her-heart in-his-right [side].

all his-life he-sought bird one small.

Hebrew is highly inflected, whereas English is not. A single word, therefore, in Hebrew may translate into many more in English. *Ukhshe'avi'ehu* means "and when I shall bring him" — six words for the one in Hebrew. The following line from Israel Efrat's "Seashells" reads:

unkik	_ofek amok_	_habo'er_	_sham_	_adom_	_bama'arav_
and the	a deep	that	there	red	in the
gash of	horizon	smolders			west

Fourteen English words are needed for the Hebrew's seven. The lines of
the translations, therefore, though usually of similar syllable count, tend
to look much longer on the page, and many translators choose to break
up the original lines. Tampering with lineation, however, is a violation
of the rhythm, one of my sacred cows. The only time I did change the
poet's original lineation was in Abba Kovner's "This Way, This Way,"
where the preservation of the poem's triangular shape seemed to me to
take precedence.

Hebrew verbs have separate conjugations for masculine and
feminine genders, and the second person pronouns, both singular and
plural, are also differentiated into masculine and feminine. Consequent-
ly, the genders of the speaker and the addressee in a poem are readily
identifiable; in English this distinction is lost. When the gender seemed
inexpendable I had to supply my own clues, as in Avigdor Ha-Me'iri's
comic counterpart to Emily Dickinson's "Because I Could Not Stop for
Death" — "That Very Night." Translated word for word, the
penultimate line would read, "Below someone whines," yet it is crucial
to the male-chauvinist bent of the poem that we know it was "a _female_
whine."

Hebrew has no neuter. A noun is either masculine (hat, man, death)
or feminine (box, woman, love). Consequently, pronoun references can
be highly ambiguous; does "he" refer back to the hat, or the man, or
death? Sometimes the ambiguity could be cleared up; at other times, it
remained. And in the English I had, occasionally, to decide whether or
not to dispense with the neuter. In a poem by Avner Trainin I decided to
leave the dove in the feminine and the cat in the masculine; I could have
made _one_ of these neuter, yet had I made _both_ neuter the reader could
not have deciphered the poem.

In Shmu'el Shatal's "Winter," the subject of the first three stanzas
appears to be a stone (feminine); yet the last line of each of these stanzas
is strangely moving. Why should the stone evoke such sorrow in the
speaker? A variant reading emerges in which the last lines each suggest,
while retaining the same pronouns (she, her), a dead woman or child. A
translator could decide to choose — the latter version is the more

poignant one; the total effect of the poem, however, stems from the give and take *between* the two versions: the dead person is like the stone now — there is no more distinction between the inanimate and the once-animate. That effect is inevitably lost in the English; I made do by offering the reader both versions.

Some Hebrew words have no English counterpart. If you look out an *eshnav* at the *shalekhet* and see crocodiles *po'arim* their mouths *litrof* the man *ha'no'el* animal skins, the translation requires phrases for each of the Hebrew words: "little window"; "state of nakedness of trees in the fall"; "spreading wide"; "to eat up alive"; and "(who is) wearing shoes (made of)." It is something like trying to draw a circle with a ruler; the tools one has to work with are just not quite right.

The difficulty is compounded when the root of a Hebrew word is repeated either in another sense or in another part of speech; often the English counterpart is simply not that flexible. The following example is from a poem by Ozer Rabin:

Yadai, asitikhen kelim
la-asiyat kelim
velo hekhiloo . . . .

In the first line *kelim* means "tools," in the second, "pottery or crockery"; and in the third line the verb *hekhiloo,* derived from the same root, means "contained." English offers no single word for all three meanings.

Conversely, because of the mysterious workings of language, an English rendering would sometimes flow better than the original. At the end of a poem by Yehudah Amikhai we read, "without / either address or recipient." English permits what the Hebrew does not, and the line can be rendered faithfully as "without / either address or addressee." The meaning here is preserved, and the single root for both words adds a momentum to the line's flow.

Hebrew does not employ capitals to designate the beginning of lines or sentences, or proper names. My decisions, therefore, tended to be intuitive. The lines of some formal poems I chose to begin with capitals throughout; a few I chose to present without any capitals. In English, capitals sometimes help, too, in resolving ambiguities; Hebrew offers no such aid. Dov Khomsky's "The Distance from Me to You" seemed on first reading a mere quibble with a friend; "I do more for you than you do for me" was the upshot of it. Only on closer inspection did I come to suspect that the speaker's quibble is with God. Capitalized pronouns would have given me the clue which I am giving the English reader.

And who knows, Khomsky's quibble *could* be with translators:

The distance from me to You isn't
equal to the distance from You to me.
The yardsticks deceive,
don't conform to
the standard.

You invade my circles
as much as You like,
any time.

You lengthen and curtail,
add and subtract and do
just as Your smoldering
eyes see fit. . . .

You see how easy it is to put a pair of horns on an artwork.

MODERN HEBREW POETRY

KHAYIM NAKHMAN BIALIK b. 1873

TAKE ME UNDER YOUR WING

Take me under your wing,
Be sister and mother to me,
Your bosom shelter for my head,
For my homeless wishes be.

And in that merciful hour of twilight,
Lean close and I'll whisper my secret chagrin —
They say, there's youth somewhere —
Where's mine?

And another mystery I'll confess
On my singed soul's behalf:
They say, there's love somewhere —
What is love?

The stars betrayed me —
I had a dream — it too beyond recall;
Now have I nothing anywhere —
Nothing at all.

Take me under your wing,
Be sister and mother to me,
Your bosom shelter for my head,
For my homeless wishes be.

1

HOMECOMING

Again before me: A ragged sage,
Face shriveled and gnarled with age,
Nomadic as a leaf, the shadow of a hay,
Over his books he seesaws away.

Again before me: A tattered hag
Knit-knitting at her woolen rags,
Her mouth is brimming oaths and drivel,
And her lips forever babble.

And still rooted to his spot
Day-dreaming, our household cat —
There by the hearth to visualize
A contract between himself and mice.

And still across the dimness strung
Threads the spider spun,
Laden with the bloated flies' corpses,
There in the far corner.

You have not altered since those days,
That ancient past has seen no change; —
Admit me, Brothers, to your clique!
Let's rot together till we reek!

A TWIG PLUMMETS

A twig plummets to the rail and to rest—
So too sleep I:
Fallen the fruit — and what possible interest
Share trunk and branch and I?

Fallen the fruit, the blossom out of mind—
Still leaves abound—
Rage a storm a single day — and lifeless
They litter the ground.

2   Khayim Nakhman Bialik

Later — and in those monstrous nights,
Sleep and peace unknown,
Alone, tossing in the dark I beat
My skull against the stone.

And again the spring shall flourish, and solitary I
To my branch shall cleave —
A barren stalk, sans bud or flower,
Or fruit, or leaf.

from AT EVENING TIME

Between clouds of fire and clouds of blood
The sun descended to the sea's flood,

And through the cloud the rays of light
Like polished spears — extremely bright.

And it quenched the land with a gentle glow
And kindled a fire in the verdant boughs.

It poured a light on the forest fronds,
And spilled a fire in the pond.

And painted gold the hilltops,
And tossed a glitter onto the crops.

And the wing of day has it turned to kiss,
Then descended live to the abyss —

When all the world in shadow dives,
Night marches on — night arrives,

And a breeze rises, blows and goes,
With a kiss it told me — what no one knows. . . .

Khayim Nakhman Bialik   3

ON THE SLAUGHTER

Ah, Heavens, intercede for me!
If a god in you there be, and he hold concourse among you —
(He has eluded me)
Then you must pray for me!
Myself — my heart is numb and no more prayer to my lips may come,
Just helplessness and hopelessness remain —
How much longer, again and again?

Executioner! Take me by the throat and cut!
Behead me like a mutt, yours the forearm and the axe —
And all the earth for me — a rack —
And we — we are the few!
My blood's a free-for-all — now hew the skull and let the death-blood
     spurt,
The blood of infant and sage upon your shirt —
That it may not ever, ever be washed clean.

And if there be Justice — Let it enter now!
But if after I'm obliterated from under the heavens
Justice make its bow
May its throne be deposed forever!
And in eternal corruption may the firmament rot;
You too, villains, go, in your wickedness,
And live and suckle in your blood.

And cursed he who says, Avenge!
Such a vengeance, of a small child's blood,
Even Satan has not fashioned yet —
May that blood pierce the abyss!
Pierce the very depths of the abyss,
And feed in darkness and undermine
All the rotted pillars of this earth.

MY FATHER

Strange was the manner of my life and wondrous were its ways,
between the pure gate and the tainted shuttled the cycle of my days,
the sacred wallowed in the gross, and innocence in squalor.
In the cave of human swine, amidst the foul pollution of the tavern,
through vapors of detested draught, and sickening mists of smoke,
behind the casks of liquor, above his yellow-parchment book
appeared to me my father's face, the skull of the martyr,
as though beheaded off its shoulders, floating in the clouds of smoke —
a countenance pale from sorrow and eyes filled red with blood;
with my eyes hung on his lips I stood in silence at his knee,
around us roared the drunkards and the gluttons splurged in their
     vomit,
monsters with leprous faces and streams of defiling tongues;
it startled the brick to listen and the windows averted their eyes.
'Only for me, in my ear alone, immaculate ear of a child,
flowed and bubbled sweetly the whisper of innocent lips,
the whisper of learning and prayer and the living words of God.
Not often could I see my father, his life with me was short;
when still quite small and tender and yet unsated of his self,
when yet depending on his mercies and the protection of his hand,
death came to take him from me, and parted us forever;
but I have tucked his likeness in my heart, it comes as I command it:
He steps as the weary oxen, in line with the harness he bears,
trudging slowly in silence, big-jointed and dull,
stubborn, controlled and indifferent, unchanging with changing time;
on cloudy days and stormy or scalding summer days,
pacing and pulling glumly the crawling stone-laden
cart of his life, along muddy roads
and sandy trails clouded with towering dust,
his neck bent in the harness, his forehead furrowed with care,
and his eyes, pools of dejection, meandering void of hope
at every highway crossing on every new main road:
From wherever he comes, won't a merciful saviour come? —
Thus would I see him always, and my spirit cringed
when he left the bosom of God each morning, the very spring of his life,
when he put his holy garments aside, his *talit* and *totafim*,

and while his eyes were still within his soul and his heart hummed like a
    magic violin,
and while his ear was far-bent still towards the distant music of the
    stars,
he went defeated, mute and confounded as though walking in his sleep
to return to the burden of his bitter days and to the labor of his hands:
to sit all day with scorpions in a reeking tavern,
to drink the breath of their mouths, be defiled by the wind of their lips.
Day after day — mount the scaffold, day after day — be cast in the lions'
    den.
And when he returned by evening soaked with pollution throughout,
repulsed, with loathing in his soul, as a man wrested out of the sewers,
the torture wrung my heart, and the mutescence of his pain was more
    than I could bear.
Ah, had I not been so little then, and void of strength,
I would have pitched my shoulder with his shoulder and put my neck
    with his,
bearing with him his sufferings and sharing with him the load;
half and half we could have shared it, I might have eased his lot —
Alas, I could do nothing and my prayer died within my breast,
while he as lonely as ever threaded his path, the weariest path,
his soul bent earthward from strain and striving,
and when the burden hurt too badly — his heart would not counter, but
    broke —
he stumbled of a sudden and died in the middle of his life.
As a beast of burden, in the middle of the road, fell my father.
Fell and rose no more.

    And in the corner of the graveyard
behind the tenements of the labourers' quarter,
in his brothers' grave, paupers and beggars
who before their time like him lie reduced to the dust of death,
washed of the grit of the world and cleansed of the filth of his days,
dressed in robes white as the morning-snow and his soul,
and wrapped in an ancient *talit* yellow as the parchment of his books
and like it all drenched with prayer and mercy,
kissed of worshiping lips and rich with holy scents,
under a cheap wooden marker, sawdust edged,

on a day in *Elul* came his body to rest,
and a brief writing at his head, inscribed by an untrained hand,
will faithfully bear him witness: "Here lies a true and honest man."

MESSAGE

The firebrand from off your altar, Prophet, cast away,
Abandon it to the rogues —
Theirs to grill their meats with, cook their casseroles
And warm the palms of their hands.
And the spark, too, from your heart cast, that it may light
The pipe bowls in their mouths,
And illumine the derision that thief-like lurks beneath mustaches,
The deception that lurks in their eyes.
Here they come, the villains, here they are —
The prayer you taught them on their tongue,
Shamming your sorrow, mouthing your dreams — yet drawn
To the stacked ruins of your altar.
And now they flock to the wreckage and burrow in the rubble heap,
Salvaging its blasted stones
And laying them for floors in their houses and onto their garden fence,
Erecting on graves their monuments.
And should they come, amidst that rubble, upon your burnt-out heart,
They'll toss it to their dogs.

Beat then against your altar, with derisive feet —
Scattering both fire and smoke.
And wipe with the swipe of a single hand the cobwebs which
Extend like violin strings throughout your heart —
Their fabric of resurrection-songs and redemptive dreams
All vanity and mere deception.
Cast them to the wind, that they may stagger, tattered and pure
     throughout the land,
On a bright day, at summer's end;
And let no thread encounter its cousin, nor single web its kin.
On the first rainy day let them perish.

Khayim Nakhman Bialik   7

Smash your iron hammer, chipped from overuse,
Useless against hearts of stone;
Smash it to smithereens, convert it into spade,
And with it dig our grave.

And be the wrath of God your message, speak it,
Without recoil —
And be your message bitter as death, and be it death itself —
It must be told.

Look, the darkness covers us, and weighs us down;
Like blindmen we stagger;
Something has befallen, and no man knows what —
None has seen, and none can say
Whether the sun rises for us or has set —
Perhaps forever.

And great the confusion all about and great all about the chaos —
And no escape.
And if we cry out in darkness and turn to pray —
What ear shall listen?
And should we invoke, cruelly, the curse of God,
On whose head shall it fall?
Or gnash our teeth, and clench an outraged fist —
On whom shall it descend?

All, all the void shall swallow, all blown in the wind,
To perish as they will.
And no succor, no subterfuge, and no device —
And the heavens speechless.
They know their trespass, vile as hell,
And in silence bear their guilt.

The burden, therefore, rests on you, Prophet of Doom:
And if you bear a message — Speak out!
And be it bitter as death, and be it death itself —
Speak out!
Why fear death — when on our shoulder its angel rides,
His bit between our teeth.
With cries of resurrection on our lips, singing hosannas of joy,
Graveward let us wend.

8   Khayim Nakhman Bialik

from IN THE CITY OF SLAUGHTER

Come with me to the City of Slaughter, come, enter its
    courtyards,
and with your own eyes see, and with your own hand feel on the
    fences
and on the trees, on the stones, on the plaster of the walls
the clotted life-blood, the hardened brains of the dead.
From there to the ruins, as you side-step each crevice,
you will pass the walls that were punctured, the stoves that were
    smashed
where the pick-point had burrowed and widened the gaps—
bare blackened stone and naked burnt brick
that look like the wide-gaping mouths of the wounds (black and
    severe)
that have no cure nor chance of healing;
and your feet will sink in feathers and stumble on piles
of fragmentary fragments and fractionate fractions, and a
    turmoil of parchments and books—
the end of inhuman effort, labor's compounded fruits;
you must not stop by the ruins, but cross over to the road
where the elm trees stand and flourish, they will spray your
    nostrils with scent,
and their buds are partly feathers and their fragrance is a
    fragrance like blood;
infuriating, spiting you, will the alien perfumes send
the tenderness of spring into your heart—nor must you sicken;
your pain shall be mocked at by seven rays from every crystal
    splinter,
while the sun with a myriad of golden arrows shall tear your
    liver to shreds.
For God has summoned the spring and the slaughter together:
The sun shone, the elm bloomed, and the butcher butchered.
You will escape and come to the courtyard, and in that courtyard
    you will find a heap—
and on that heap these were slaughtered: A Jew and his dog.
One axe beheaded them, on the same leavings were they thrown
and in the mingled blood of both will the swine snoop and
    wallow;

Khayim Nakhman Bialik 9

tomorrow the rain will come and carry it into a ditch—
the blood will not cry from the sewers and waste-piles
for it will lose itself in the chasms or quench a sapling's thirst—
then all will be as nothing, and all will be as it was.
And you will climb up to the garrets and stand there in the
    semidark—
the dread of death's bitters still floats in the muted gloom
and out of the corner shadows and all the unlit gaps
look, eyes, eyes are staring at you dumbly.
They are the ghosts of the "holy," lost, disconsolate souls,
into one corner, under one roof have they dumbly crowded.
Here the axe had reached them and here they returned again
to seal with their looks, for the very last time,
the sorrow of their cruel deaths and all the weariness of their
    existence;
huddled together, trembling and fearful, from their corner
they question their hurt in silence and their eyes are asking:
    Wherefore?
And who but God alone on earth could stand to bear this
    stillness?
You will look up and find that even the tiles of the roof are
    hushed,
glum and muted, and you will turn to ask the spiders;
eyewitnesses all, and living, they will tell you what took place:
There's the story of the belly that was slit and stuffed with
    feathers,
there's the story of nostrils and nails, of skulls and hammers,
there's the story of men who were slaughtered and dead were
    hanged with rope;
then there's the story of the baby found sleeping
with his dead mother's nipple held cold in his mouth,
and then there's the story of the child torn to pieces that died
    crying, "Mother!"—
His eyes too are here, demanding a reckoning from me.
This that and more the spider can tell you,
stories that bore through the brain and can deaden
your spirit and soul with a death complete and forever—
you will restrain yourself and stifle the roar in your throat

10   Khayim Nakhman Bialik

and before it rises bury it deep in your heart
and run from there, and out—and find the world as ever,
and the sun as yesterday and the day before, squandering its
   gold on the earth.

Leave now, and return again at dusk
to catch the final act of mourning, to find the souls
just wakened by fear in the morning—slumbering again by
   night;
worn and weary with weeping they stand now in the dark—
their lips are still moving, praying—but the roof of the heart is
   sealed,
and without a spark of hope in the heart and without a gleam of
   light in the pupil
the hand gropes in the darkness, seeking a crutch—and finding
   none . . .
Thus smokes the wick when the oil is gone,
thus pulls the aging horse whose powers are no more.
Had their woes but left them one fable's consolation
to revive their spirits and support them in their near old age!
The fast is over now, they have read, "And the Lord ceased . . ."
   they have prayed, "Oh, Answer Us . . ."—yet why
is the congregation lingering?—Will they read "Lamentations"
   too?
No! The speaker is now mounting the platform,
now he opens his mouth, stammers and breathes epithets,
spills nothings and whispers quotations over their open
   wounds,
and from his mouth he cannot raise one word of God,
nor kindle one tiny spark in their hearts;
and old and young, the chosen flock is poised
some listening and yawning, some shaking their heads.
The mark of death is on their brows and their hearts are sterile.
Dead is their spirit, gone is their vigor, and their God has left
   them.

And now what will you do here, Man? Rise and escape to the
   desert—
carry with you the cup of trembling,

tear your soul there in a half-score shreds,
feed your heart to your impotent fury,
shed your tear on the skull of rocks,
send out your bitter roar—and let it be lost in the storm.

SHA'UL CHERNIKHOVSKY b. 1875

VULTURE! VULTURE IN YOUR MOUNTAINS

Vulture! Vulture in your mountains, vulture in your mountains flies!
Light and slow—as though a moment merely floating,
Floating/sailing azure seas; to the paean in the heart
Of heaven—skies—attuned, silent he curves through scalding light.

Vulture! Vulture in your mountains, vulture in your mountains flies!
Stiff of gait, of sluggish limb, black his feathers, wide his wings;
Taut as from bow the arrow flies, the vulture circumscribes his arc;
Tracks the traces of his prey in field and crevice from on high.

Vulture! Vulture in your mountains, vulture in your mountains flies!
Coasting/gliding and, by feat of magic, did not bend a wing,
Froze—one second, and the next—a tremor through his limbs,
Suddenly a certain shudder—and toward the clouds he climbs.

Vulture! Vulture in your mountains, vulture in your mountains flies!
Light and slow—as though—a moment merely floating . . .
Landscape, vulture in your mountains—across your face the ominous
    dark
Of a giant's wings is passing, caressing the mountains of God.

ZALMAN SHNE'UR b. 1886

SNOW SONG

Hey! who's pulverized the sky!
Here it comes, bit by bit;
Integrated the streets—
Blessed be the changer of seasons!

Fields were there, tell us, where?
Gardens, too—gone—whereto?
Just white, white, white,
All the colors hibernate.

Snow and laughter on every face.
The sleighs go by—in silhouette;
And in the chaos of the feathers' white
The tops of the steeples liquify.

The snow rebounds—and in its dance
One black raven's swept aside;
Caw, caw, caw . . . Oh, raven, raven,
It's white, all white!

14

AVIGDOR HA-ME'IRI b. 1890

SILENCE

The sun is red. It naps.
So too rest I.
Silence.

My eyes are fixed at the heights.
Above me a pair of ravens.
Silence.

An earthworm in my brain.
Contented.
Asleep.
Silence.

The sun is red. It naps.
So too rest I.
Silence.

THAT VERY NIGHT

Someone knocks at my window,
calls with a musical leer:
—Hello, Death is here.

I recoil, but rise, smiling
(never reveal your fear):
—Wait, we'll go together.

The teasing voice says merrily,
a spring-bell loud and clear:
—Hurry, or you won't get there.

I fall then rise and hurry
and Vega looks down from the sky:
—No, no, just wait, by and by.

Silence. On a fall night, night of my birth,
I quickly leave my place,
—Come on then, let's race.

And so we two race, laughing, aloft.
Below a female whine deplores:
—He forgot to shut the door.

from WRITTEN IN A PUBLIC RESTAURANT

Dumpy and obese—a woman
cleans the tables in the restaurant.

Proudly she stalks up and down,
flirting almost,
wet rag in her right hand,
golden bracelet on her left.

And when she wipes a table
sometimes the bracelet sprinkles the rag
with its gold.

INTERSTICE IN THE DEEP

The inner deep of the sea has an interstice
underneath all the waves
glowing like phosphor.

There I and you asleep with the rest,
each mouth against ear and each ear
filled with listening.

And every word we speak here is so drowsy yet,
that it will cock its head a moment
and release a ray of light—

Then it finds its way back to the same
ear, the same mouth,
to the same sleep.

THE BIRD OF MY BEING

Now the bird of my being sings
only when I shut window and door,
and lower the shades.

Now between me and the world
the thread is so thin,
a mere wink will expel it.

They say the bird sings
more sweetly
when blinded.

NARCISSUS

A wound in the heart won't redden like a rose
nor be moistened by blood—
itself is all the heart, is all the soul.

Huddled within itself, altogether bent
upon its own tip—
tip kisses tip

Like a pair of birds on a thin wire of spring.

Or else in the deep closure of a well
alongside a mirror square and dim
it sits and looks and wonders—

What joy loves itself as much as pain?

SEASHELL

All the flat sea lies grey before me
and above my head the contortions of the clouds
and the gash of a deep horizon that smolders there red in the west—
like slivers of flesh on a spit—
a single and singular seashell in which I am locked.

I lean on the fence and wonder: When God
lifts the All to His ear
shall He listen only to the voice of the vast sea,
or also to me, also to me,

Since there are moments when He and I
exchange places and I hear His voice.

CERTAIN DAYS

Certain days objects evaporate and are gone
and I float as a blind man floats

in the tune his long white cane
draws from the cobblestones.

Certain days I stalk a world-not-world
and all my senses stagger,

and the world sheds its clothes and tries
my soul on against its naked torso.

THE HEART WILL HAVE ITS WAY

Merry tongues in the lit fireplace
and undisrupted peace in the house—suddenly
a sigh escapes

Israel Efrat   19

Escapes and crashes in the crimson dark
pleads before shadow after warm shadow on the wall
till it exits to the cold night—

While we gaze in the undisrupted silence
at the tongues of the flame.

MARINE BIOLOGY

There's a sea beneath a sea beneath a sea
where all the fishes, utterly blind,
are swathed in shawls of splendor.

And by and by on the way back up
the eyes open, the splendor is shed
onto the sightless ocean bed.

There's a sea beneath a sea beneath a sea—
those delicate silks and glowing hues
only the silent waves perceive.

URI TSVI GREENBERG b. 1894

THE CUTTING OFF

Lo and behold, on a cloudless day,
Amid the fragrance of all growing things,
While the birds fly—as on a single wing . . .
Woe to the beholder who in his hands did not seize
the berries of his eyes—and wring!

Even the birds themselves don't know who cut off their wing.

Lo and behold, as they fly through the air
tilting to one side . . .
Not even blood dripping, nor memory of when a pair
Of wings per bird made passage fair.

Ah hearts yearning from hither to yon—
Now have no more yonder.
The Lord's command as in a dream that wing has sundered
And stamped his name on the stump.

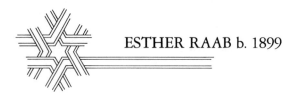

ESTHER RAAB b. 1899

YOU ARE THE MAN— . . .

You are the man—
I'm ever so proud of you,
who knew how to subdue
all the crocodiles opened wide their maws
to swallow me;
you are the man
who on the stone slopes of my cliffs
has sown a smile
and the loneliness of a mutt lost in the dark
has bravely shared with me.

LIKE A BIRD DEAD IN THE STREAM . . .

Like a bird dead in the stream
you floated towards me.
Your eyes extinguished/stagnant
and out of the muted gold
still whispering briefly;
your arms weary,
dripping their sadness.
Over us the meager olive,
pale shadows at our feet.

MY ARMS ARE RAISED TOWARDS YOU . . .

My arms are raised towards you,
towards the modicum of light
your glance still holds for me,
and you flash your teeth
at my jaundiced tender flesh;
and be this flesh cast in the fields
and a vulture circling above it—
still my arms are raised towards you,
towards the modicum of light
your glance still holds for me.

TODAY I AM MODEST AS A BEAST . . .

Today I am modest as a beast,
sprawled out like a drenched meadow;
by a small fat hand shall I lead my life
towards compassion and towards the children.
Today any stranger and penitent
may approach me—
like the round-about rain will splatter
the minimal gifts of my heart;
and already I bear the morrow—
a burden hermetic
and once more spurting
away towards the unknown.

SELF-PORTRAIT

If you should find my bones after thousands of years
if they should say, "A find!"—
here's the key:
Bones long/straight,

bones of candor
and a wide step
down dear homeland ways.
Skull round/clean
for the smooth thought.
The heart the worms have eaten
at orchard-blossom time
and longings-never-came
or were lost.
Lovelessly . . .

ETRUSCAN STATUE

Your heavy eyes
smile on me
from across thousands of years
your mouth—that knows
how to command its legions
and kiss the women's lips—
half open
another moment
and speech will burst
from your lips—spread wide
and full and wise—
what will your idiom be?
flashing cropped lightning bolts,
hair-raising ones?
or singing soft and sad—
to fall like an autumn leaf
and sink deep into the heart?
your mustache is combed to perfection
and your beard well kempt—
pointed and brusque—
your neck is straight and firm
and your face narrow and alive—
your noble, your taut being

I sense altogether—
only don't descend from your pedestal
tonight, Thousand-Year-Old,
for I dread your touch.

AVRAHAM SHLONSKY b. 1900

A CITIZEN'S DISSERTATION
ON HIS NEIGHBORHOOD

My apartment building has 5 stories
and all its windows yawn straight across,
like sundry faces in a mirror.

70 bus lines traverse my town
all filled to stifling with body stench.
And they travel
and they travel
and they travel to the metropolis,
as if one couldn't die of boredom here, too,
right in my neighborhood.

For though my neighborhood is very small,
it still contains the births and the demises,
and whatever comes in between,
of any city in the world—
even babies, miraculously twirling their hoops,
and 3 movie houses.
If the boredom of my own house had not sufficed,
I'd have gone to one of these.

My apartment building has 5 stories—
but for her who leapt from the window opposite
3 were quite enough.

MIRIAM YALAN-SHTEKLIS b. 1900

from PRAYER TO BE SUNG

Padlock your garden, my dear,
For night is near, and night is black,
Padlock your garden!
How can I padlock my garden, my dear?
When the tall, illuminated skies are rose—
How can I padlock my garden?

Padlock your window, my dear,
For night is near, and night is black, and the storm, the blizzard
     is near,
Padlock your window!
How can I padlock my window, my dear,
When clods of damp earth yield up their scent,
And the voices of men sound from afar—
How can I padlock my window?

Padlock your door, my dear,
For the black night is near, and storm and blizzard are near,
And robbers stalk down hidden paths;
Watch them approach.
Padlock your door!
How can I padlock my door, my dear?
And my brother stalks down hidden paths,
Stalks poor, impoverished, shelter-starved,
Shelter for his weary head—
How can I padlock my door?

Padlock your heart, my very own,
For cruel night has fallen, and the storm has struck,
And the villain struts in your garden, your house,
And you are alone;
Padlock your heart, my dear,
Lest he wound your heart, my very own!
How can I padlock my heart, my dear?
And I cast in the sea both lock and bar,
And my heart remained—an open, always open city;
Neither wall, nor tower, nor sentries there,
And in its gates come light and night, and storm with sorrow,
And my very own brother, poor, impoverished traveler,
The villain and the stranger;
Yes, my very own, the villain and the stranger,
The cruel stranger.

And I blessed my fate, contented,
And said, "Amen,"
And my heart remained wide open.

YOKHEVED BAT-MIRIAM b. 1901

JUST AS YOU SEE ME, THAT'S HOW I AM . . .

Just as You see me, that's how I am:
no eye-shadow, rouge; neither make-up nor charm,
but barbaric, perverse, and extremely rude—
that's how I would come to stand before You.

So and so many feet is the sum of my height,
so and so many years my lease on this earth.
An extra measure for my spirit's flight
when it bursts from its cage and wanders without word.

And my chatter won't transport me to heaven,
a chatter turned stammer with sudden dismay.
I don't know how to address You, even,
I who am dying with each passing day.

With each passing day, like a dream's illusion
both land and sea still rise and shine,
as whitewashed highways from nought to nothing
will tug at the azure of the sky and the brine.

And I've already ceased to exist, long hence,
my destination waves from across the border.
Is the remission of sin, of penance, revenge,
remorse and reward not in order?

And here I'm before You, just as I am,
barbaric, perverse, fuming bitterly.
And a bare, harsh lament envelops me
for myself who won't be the I of me . . .

LEVI BEN-AMITTAI b. 1901

ON A FALL NIGHT

In loneliness and distance how faint the lights.
A star amid clouds crossing the skies.

A cock crows in rage and crows again—
And haughtily answers him a nearby man.

The valley asleep, in leaves and mud;
No place to go—no wish to set out.

Yet in this gloom we stayed on silently:
Lights and star, the cock and I.

MY SOUL IN THE PALM OF YOUR HAND

I put my soul in the palm of your hand,
like a fledgling furry and warm
that fell from its nest,
the nest of a bird.

Shall I be your plaything,
fledgling in a vicious-naïve boy's palm
who found it on his way?

Surely you will lay
it back in the nest
by the mother's wing
from which it was plucked,
and for which it blindly yearns.

30

THE DIGGER FOR GOLD

If the earth won't yield me gold
I'll go dig in the sky's craters
From star to star untold
I'll traverse the gold like water.

If the earth won't interpret my dream
And my dream like wounded loiter,
I'll wake from the grave my mother's shade—
Whose dreams destroyed her.

And ask my mother of the Land of the Dead,
Whether death also chaos dread?
And whether death too be sometimes sad?
And has he made a friend of God?

Or is death merely carnage and flame,
Eternity's scorn in the mouth of a worm?
And is he blind and deaf and dumb—
And mindless?

IN THE NIGHT BIRDS FELL

In the night birds fell from the nest,
And trees trembled in the night.
And the great lives became little
And cried to survive.

Perhaps there was nothing anymore in the sky.
Perhaps there had never been anything in the sky.
And only someone,
                    Like a bird which fell from the nest,
Fancied to find anything in the sky.

And the crying was reassured by its essence,
And the tears reassured by themselves.

In the night,
                    Always in the night,
Rages a monstrous storm
And throttles the heart of the branches.
And the branches dimly recall that their heart aches.
And someone like a bird which fell from the nest
Like a broken branch,
Someone who does not know who he is, who he is, who he is—
Falls also.

A CERTAIN MAN

A certain man recites his song in silence
between window, walls, and rectangular door.
Pitifully narrow his confines
and infinite his mind.

An ancient spider suddenly ensnares him.
Two are its faces: death and weary old night.
But the man who is swathed in its clutches
is erudite.

A certain man's room is confounded
between his flesh and reflections and Eternity,
and sundry things joyless and tearless.

And the sky over him is lofty—
an all-embracing brightness.
A certain man recites his song in silence.

32   Avraham Khalfi

SUBURB

Street puddle—
a muddy river facing a sea of rain.
A restless image—yellowed portrait.
Who tonight will pen a poem
with rainbow-colored ink?

A suburb curved its alleyways
to the far horizon.
It's fall here. Mere fall.
And dreams—are shards of pottery.
But a tree stays.

Drained.
Scorched by flame.
Doesn't know why it's a tree—
and only in daydreams will it sprout its greenery.

FLOWERS PINK WITH EBONY . . .

Flowers pink with ebony
eye
incline their heads above the vase.

From my window
that faces a display-window street
I dispatched a dove.

She is tired from traversing the city
vast in its distance between man and man.

Midway in her journey will she surely drop.

TONIGHT THE MOON FELL . . .

Tonight the moon fell
from its shining-place

Avraham Khalfi   33

and didn't bequeath its light to
a single star above.

It is the dream of a man who fancied that he fell,
he too,
and in his house an antique lamp
from those other days
and those other nights went out.

A GOLDEN-GREEN DAWN . . .

A golden-green dawn
tinged with a violet hue
spreads over the Mediterranean Sea.

A very early morning
hour or very late
at night.

The wine hurts.
Something green or golden in it, or
violet.

A drunken dawn. And as though our hands
touched its edges.

SHIN SHALOM b. 1904

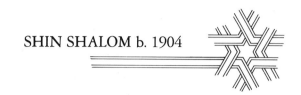

EVENINGS, WHEN SPARKS

Evenings, when sparks
Kindle the mountain
Sets one out of me
For far away lands.

His mantle is a cloud,
His amazement the sea.
I hark after his spirit
With grasses and awe.

I cry without utterance,
He winks without stir.
And the echo of the steps of his distance
Languish yet in me . . .

MARVEL DOWN . . .

Marvel down my heart, my heart down marvel,
day borne to day, night upon night unravel.
Shed your clothes and into the felt and vibrant dive—
every touch revelation, every vision alive.

Road follow my heart, heart follow the road,
man is a god on it, the driven forgiven on it.
Wherever you wander, wherever you bide
the secret rests with you, the wind by your side.

Verse release my heart, heart release the verse;
to the light without end, to the infinite worth
raise your glass and drink to sorrow and to mirth,
embracing life and embracing death.

ALL'S NOT THAT SIMPLE

All's not that simple in the yards of these lodgings,
From each of these stories windows are watching;
On the faded walls and the desolate pavements
Each hour, passing hour will leave its engraving.

All's not that simple within the walls of these spaces;
Something's implied in the stance of their book cases
And the heavy drapes and the bed turned down
Kneel under the yoke, kneel under wisdom's burden.

And in all of these buildings are those dark flights
Where in the morning descend and climb at night
Secrets that keep silent and lock the door—
These my soul goes out to, these my soul prays for.

YONATAN RATOSH b. 1909

A MILLION

in the past
  —just as now—
  there were a million women
          in this
       —innocent or whoring—
       world

and even now
  there certainly are a million and more women
          in this
       —wise or foolish—
       world

and only one is absent today somehow
         very much
and the million seems suddenly wanting
         so very much
there's simply nothing left to choose from—

and if
  a fool or sage
  or whoremaster
or naif
will change places with me—

wholeheartedly
  let him take—for my part—all of them
           to the last

37

the whole of that amorous
              million
    I somehow need
              only that particular
                  one
I'm somehow prepared
              to make do—

NATAN ALTERMAN b. 1910

RED RIDINGHOOD

While our savage day is wiped like a tear
Off cities and forests, the month and the year,
Down the path goes Red Ridinghood
To gather wild flowers in the wood.

And following her are cow and goose
And hobbling cat on a cane—
Like a legend lost, like an ancient tune,
Like the ghost of a smile forgotten and gone.

And the coming years stand far apart
And our befuddlement triples pointlessly
And the naked moon, as at the start,
Is sucking his thumb on his Father's knee.

And we keep silent. The turf's down
Titillates with lashes of green . . .
We close our eyes—then look again
And dark has enveloped the tree's crown.

SUMMER NIGHT

Stillness whispers from afar.
The blade's white in the eye of the cat.
Night. Deep night. The heavens quiet.
In diapers—the stars.

39

A broad, broad time. Two thousand, the heart has struck.
Dew veils our lashes like rendezvous,
A streetlamp's gilded whip subdues
Negro slaves the length of the dock.

Dim, yet alive, a summer breeze roams,
Its lips traveling down the garden's shoulder.
Verdant malice. Lights and distrust moulder.
A treasure sizzles in the black foam.

And up yonder, with ravenous moan,
Its eyes gold-plated, a whole town
Evaporates with rage, in the billowing stone
Of its towers and its domes.

TONIGHT

Tonight.
The estrangement of these walls.
A battle of silence in adjacent flesh.
The evanescent life
of a candle.

Only a disconsolate whisper, like a chill wind,
slipped by along these shattered fences
and caressed the fainting pavements and rocked
bridges like a sequence of cradles.

A shadow crosses the empty square; is gone.
Only the thunder of its steps continues.
Please not to forget, to forget, Eternal Dust,
the feet of the men who have trod you.

Tonight.
The tension in these walls.
A voice wakes and demands. A voice answers and ceases.
A strange caress. Light of a forced smile.
The life and death
of a candle.

40   Natan Alterman

Then the moon coats with masks of wax
the icy stare, the window, the landscape,
the market place resting, paralyzed with stroke,
in the extended monster-arms of carts and cranes.

THE FOUNDLING

My mother laid me by the fence,
Wrinkle-faced and silent on my back.
And I looked up at her as from a well,
Till she fled like a deserter.
   And I looked up at her, as from a well,
   And the moon was held high like a candle.

Yet before the dawn lit the sky that night,
I got up, for the time was ripe—
And returned to my mother's home like a ball
That returns to the player's side.
   And returned to my mother's home like a ball
   And round her neck threw my shadowy arms.

She from her bosom, not caring who sees,
Tore me away like a leech.
Yet with nightfall I returned again,
And this became our ritual:
   At nightfall I returned again,
   And nightly she yields to duty and to claim.

And the doors of her dreams open wide to me
And no man but I in the dream.
For our souls' attachment remained as taut
As a bow, from the day of my birth.
   For our souls' attachment remained as taut
   And never to be sold and never to be bought.

Wherefore the Lord has never removed
Me from my mother's squealing heart
And I—who was severed unweaned—

Natan Alterman 41

Haven't been weaned and shall never let go.
　　And I who was severed unweaned
　　Enter her house and lock the door.

She's aged in my cage, impoverished, dwindled
And her face wrinkled like mine.
Then my tiny hands clothed her in white
Like a mother her living child.
　　Then my tiny hands clothed her in white
　　And I carried her off without telling her where.

And laid her down by the fence
Attentive and silent on her back.
And she looked up at me smiling, as from a well,
And we knew that the battle was done.
　　And she looked up at me smiling as from a well,
　　And the moon was held high like a candle.

LE'AH GOLDBERG b. 1911

THE TREE CELEBRATES THE RIVER

He who has borne my golden fall
My blood swept away with my leaves,
Who shall see my spring's recall
With the season's reprieve,

Brother River, forever lost,
Daily renewed, both changed and not at all,
Brother Stream between his banks
Flowing like me from spring to fall.

For I am the bud and I am the fruit,
I what's to come and I what's gone,
I am the barren trunk,
And you—my clock and my song.

KHAMSIN OF NISAN

Of course I know, this day's without compare
Yet nothing happened, nothing changed
And nothing good nor evil occurred
To set it apart from other days.

The sun merely exudes its jasmine,
The stone merely has the heartbeat's voice,
The sunset merely is tinted orange,
The sand merely like lips that kiss.

43

How to recall it, impersonal, blunt,
How to preserve its sudden grace,
How, looking back, believe that once
Each scent and quiver was blood of my blood?

For every tree was a trembling sail,
And the silence had eyes like a girl's,
And tears held the fragrance of buds,
And the city's name was my love's.

FROM MY MOTHER'S HOUSE

My mother's mother died
in her youth, and her daughter
could not recall her face. Her likeness, engraved
on my grandfather's heart
was erased from the world of images
with his death.

Only her mirror remained in the house,
receding with time into its silver setting.
And I, her pallid grandchild, who resemble her not at all,
look into it, daily, as into
a lake that hides its treasures
under water.

Deep inside, behind my own face,
I see a young woman
rosy-cheeked and smiling,
the required wig on her head.
She places
an elongated earring into the lobe, threads it
through the tiny puncture in the tender flesh
of her ear.

Deep inside, behind my own face, glimmers
the bright gold of her eyes.

44   Le'ah Goldberg

And the mirror perpetuates the family
tradition:
that she had been most lovely.

ELUL IN GALILEE

1.
One hundred silences and not a single tear.
The mountains speechless.
We stepped exhausted in the thistles
and the wind blew southward.

At the crossroad stood an ancient olive,
lonesome like you from root to crown,
its aged face abandoned to perennial wind;
we stepped defeated among the thistles
and night fell.

2.
Speak well of me in an autumn such as this
among scorched mountain tops,
when the snakes emerge from their refuge
and glide mute and pray for rain;
when the tree tires of bearing fruit
and all the weary resemble it.

HEAT SPELL IN VENICE
(*from* The Italian Poems)

Thus has he forsaken me, the god unknown
in a strange city, amid the canals,
the hotel room like a convent cubicle.
The window open. The hour noon.

Scattered on the roof opposite lies broken glass
and the rhyme fragment—"Lord, take us back to yesterday!"

In the muck of the greening wave
noiselessly crawls the gondola.

A plump pigeon passes slow of step.
The dust of centuries turns the sky pale.
The heat rises, and facing the canal
the lions are seized with sleep.

OPEN WINDOW IN FLORENCE
(*from*　The Italian Poems)

And sun on the roof, and the memory of Fiesole,
and a bell deep as the sky's abyss,
and on the pigeons' wings a message of feasting and peace
and the soft smile of the Messiah.

And in the tranquil heavens it's written that
the day will come when on the carpet of light
in his golden glow the keeper of the gates
will lay the key at my feet.

ON THE HAZARDS OF SMOKING

Rainy morning. Don't get up. Don't even smoke.
Don't read too much. Isn't it a queer spring!
Isn't it a queer spring. Darkness in the morning as though . . .
Don't read too much. Isn't it a cloudy spring!

Once you were a complainer. Did it help? Did it bring back your dead?
What pain in the flesh, in the poem, in the papers, in the Song of Songs.
Limits to wisdom? Maybe. Just as well we learned meanwhile
Not to wake the neighbors, not to trouble friends.

Rainy morning. Don't get up. The night passed peacefully.
The night passed. And now—isn't it a cloudy spring.
Morning like night. All right. Only the stillness stifles.
Isn't it an oppressive spring! I told you: Don't smoke.

46　Le'ah Goldberg

GAVRI'EL PREIL b. 1911

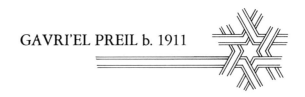

FISHERMEN

All day long the rain would not desist
from repeating its grey fables.
All day long the wind would not desist
from leafing through them.
Yet in the Central Library
a southern climate prevails,
and it's as though fishermen sat
on the banks of a
chanting stream:

In their hands glitters their catch—
while overhead,
cloud upon cloud is devoured.

SHINING THING

I have often sung of the snow
for the bones of man
are like the melting snow.
I have praised the sun
for the bones of man
glow just like it.
But when I drew pictures
a rainy day saw them first,

and when I put letters down
the cloud would give them birth—
So it is with every shining thing.

LAKES

Whitening striations bruise this lake of ice.
Winter-merry specters stop and go upon it;
From somewhere time the blind, the smoldering
And vital spat them out.

The corresponding lake above traversed by wounds of light and cloud.

And it—time's eternal testament and bedfellow—

A circling plane's tip takes aback, or a strange moon
Ploughs through its waves.

The blue knives of the ice shall be
Like flowers in the memory,
Snow-tints shall sled in it
Like silver and like fleece:

Ere the tune of the lake shall peter out
And the known world vanish.

BEYOND THE IMAGINARY GARDEN

My erstwhile glance, once cast at a river,
is no longer mine, the unrivered, now.
I became, if not a patient stone, forever reconciled,
then a tree that has grown as though from sluggish habit
and forgot the hope of the tallness of youth.

My erstwhile glance, once cast at a mountain,
is no longer mine, the nonmountainous, now.
I became, if not a valley sinking into the depths,
then a night train passing nonstop
and refusing to admit the existence of stations.

I became like a wasteland beyond the imaginary garden.

DOV KHOMSKY b. 1913

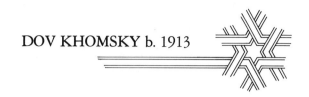

SUNBEAMS DIAGONALLY

Sunbeams diagonally poke
among branches of a tree that dreams
a terrifying dream. A wild
shadow gives itself airs
as though it too were tree.

Morsels of severed darkness
and dazed, suspect
sparks
speed hither and yon—
between laden earth
and a flickering,
elusive sky.

Silence chafes silence like
a couple of stones.

A CLOUDLESS MORNING

A cloudless morning
omits all that isn't
essential to casting its gold.

skips a pitfall
real and imagined.

rips windows open
for miracle and awe.

licks wounds of nettle and thorn.

YOUR EYES THAT GAZE

Your eyes that gaze on this and that:
an ominous dark and oppressive light.

Build your house
and open its many windows wide
to all your landscapes forgotten
but still engraved
on all the holy tablets.

Your eyes that gaze inward,
your eyes that gaze out—
expendable joy
and excessive grief.

PAPER FLOWERS

Paper flowers
on both sides of the street
that sprouts in your heart,
that sprouts all by itself.

In all the shop windows,
one upon another and another
both waking and in dreams.

Your imaginary birds
hop about your cage.
You add on bar
after bar for fear
they too should suddenly
escape.

Paper flowers—
your imaginary birds
sip from their splendor.

50   Dov Khomsky

THE DISTANCE FROM ME TO YOU

The distance from me to You isn't
equal to the distance from You to me.
The yardsticks deceive,
don't conform to
the standard.

You invade my circles
as much as You like,
any time.

You lengthen and curtail,
add and subtract and do
just as Your smoldering
eyes see fit.

I am watched. You watch
through my walls and shuttered
windows.

THE MOON DIPS IN THE PUDDLE'S FLOW

The moon dips in the puddle's flow
on the silent street's slope (the rain has stopped).
It splashes, mischievous and playful as a tot.

In the sky impetuous cloudlets float.
The moon steps silent and slow.
Was it suddenly crossed by the road?

Take your pick: Moon above or below.

EVEN ON THE LOVELIEST OF NIGHTS

Even on the loveliest of nights stars
die suddenly—and no one knows

Dov Khomsky   51

it's swallowed them. And no one weeps
and nòne laments. The survivors
shed their gold—capricious and flickering.

Even on the loveliest of nights the bats
slip by, black in their cunning and flight.

The striped horizon
crouches low as a curling snake.

Breezes gnaw at the silence,
gnaw mercilessly.

Even on the loveliest of nights—

SHMU'EL SHATAL b. 1913

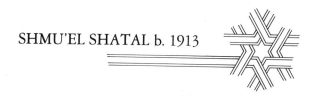

WINTER

Stone stark naked
stone cold as death
the dust fallen on its eyes.

Stone sheaving against the wind
made heavy, cruel by the wind
grass grew on its cheeks.

Stone toying with wind
conceived and bore the wind
from its eyes a pale flower.

I pluck.

WINTER
(alternate translation)

Stone stark naked
stone cold as death
the dust fallen on her eyes.

Stone sheaving against the wind
made heavy, cruel by the wind
grass grew—on her cheeks.

53

Stone toying with wind
conceived and bore the wind
a flower more pale than her eyes.

I pluck.

THE MOUNTAIN'S SIDE

Was it a fragment of rock or of cloud
that tore my flesh on either side
and swept up the poppies breathing fiery on my lips

Or perhaps that morning
I broke loose from under the mountain's ruminations
and took a step, a single one, to the valley
to let poppies that sprouted flock on flock
play between my toes

Poised here am I still
like a rib in the mountain's side
holding my breath
scarred and exposed to my very stones

In the valley of silent poppies.

BETWEEN YOU AND ME

No one noticed it at the housewarming of our new home—
even the architect said it wasn't a dangerous crack—
sooner or later the unexpected appears in every
building, he said—
                    and in the building's mute language shows
the impossible strain of such persistent tension.

Even if the ground sank under us
                    and with it sank the foundations,

even if the foundations did sink
                    the ground unable to bear them—
it's still our house
                    either suspended or aslant—
a building isn't a piece of glass—
even if the crack widens and grows as the years pass—
even the architect said every building's fated,
sooner or later,
to diverge from the original plan—
repository for memories' roots that cling
to the cracks of the planks of another day—
temple for mosses that cushion the fissures of time

Why are you silent? Why won't you tell me it's O.K.—
even the architect did say

ZELDA b. 1914

BLACK ROSE

Could my longings have
created the black rose you
gave me in the dream
or did your longings flower-like push up
from the hidden world
into my dream?
And why did I ask you suddenly
for earrings,
something I had never done while
you were in the land of the living?

FAINT ECHO

This bough here in my vase
with its scented, yellow blossoms
has detected a faint echo
of the clamor of summer
in my soul.
An echo
of that summer muted
on a bitter day.

56

HERE'S A WOMAN LIVED TO AN EXTREME OLD AGE

Here's a woman lived to an extreme old age
without a remnant of fire's madness
or summer's sap.
Her thin flesh has evaporated
and gleams in the dark like an ancient tale—
stirring revulsion in corpulent men
and in the green leaves of the mulberry.

AN ENCHANTED BIRD

When the tender body
is about to fall
and divulges its fear of the end
to the soul
the lowly tree of habit which dust
has devoured suddenly
sprouts greenery.
For the scent of the void shall deck it
in comely splendor
and its crown shall house
an enchanted bird.

THE MERRY IMAGINATION

For the merry imagination has a secret key
of simpletons and clods
that opens the sciences' ivory doors
and it enters
their castles in the air,
strolls through the dark
acrawl with formulae—
and whistles astonished there
like an errand boy.

THE ACACIA TREE

The bright-green acacia tree, decked with the fragrance
it lifted from the plains below
remains faithful to itself
on Jerusalem's heights—
free of all melancholy
it toys
with tiny golden wreaths,
revives
the pliant me in me
when it gets burnt.

DAVID ROKE'AKH b. 1916

THE FLEETING TOO

The fleeting too rushes to look in mirrors,
in those eyes
deeper than the eyes of the sea.
Butterflies
that drew near the flame
revived in gardens of fire.

CHILDHOOD

We grew like vines and matured like them
in the sadness of adolescence.
We climbed the wall
to hunt for the curving horizon
in the conspiracy of our sinful eyes
and on our bodies beat the fall
with energies bred by desire.

We saw the land defoliation-bound
and enemy troops
invading the vineyard
with martial cries.

That first surrender extinguished a secret spark
in the light of our startled eyes.

THEN

Then
when I didn't know myself
I tossed a coin in the air
to see how things would befall.
Now that my love will rule me
and I have no coins anymore
I am like one stranded on the roof
while the fire laps at the ladder's rungs.

EVERY CITY

Every city has a river traversing its dreams.
As the winter deepens, visions are etched in the frost.
At the freezing stream the willows of the bank will marvel.
And a beneficent snow falls like cherry blossoms on the mass below.

A city's misdemeanor—purity, transparency of the upper regions;
decked in jewels it mounts the bridge and dreams.

THE SPRING OF CITIES

The spring of cities is wildflowers
on the market's bargain stands.
The deep blue of cornflowers
across from the envious yellow of ragwort.

The spring of cities is the infrequent wind
whose blowing exhales the best of scents
of almond blossom and of lilac blooms.

The spring of cities is the dew
that covers the dreams
of astonished maidens
whom dawn awakens
and whom the meaning of fantasies escapes.

60   David Roke'akh

AMIR GILBO'A b. 1917

AGAINST THE WIND

As we stood at the cliff's edge
A great wind came up
And everyone drew back.
Only I seized the mallet
Stowed there for ages
And began throttling the rock.

And the wind replied: So be it!

IN THE DARK

I put out my hands before me, into the dark
And my fingers begged for light
Atremble with the fear of uncertainty.

I gathered then these fingers
Inward towards the palm,
And they began to whimper softly
Like pups against their mother's dugs
Infinitely reassured
In the clenched fist's circle.

Then came the dawn.

A RED AND BLUE SONG

You passed as through snow; and through snow you passed.
And bears gave you chase. Papa; mama; baby bear.
And you ran with all your might, thought all was lost.
And tossed in your eyes—the terror of the years.

And here you are. Years have passed. Have passed.
Gone the handsome bears. Or will they reappear?
In our garden tonight the pine branches snapped
And the trees shall run blood and tears.

So it goes. We're young still.
But in memory—a thousand years.
Look, all the ghosts beyond your window sill
Form a single line. None is far or near.

THE RIDERS' HORSES

The riders' spears touched heaven
and the horses prided themselves on it.
Yet I drew horses proud and erect
without riders
without spears.
And my horses bore no harness
running wild on paper and ceiling and floor.
And later, loose with me in the meadow,
they sprouted wings.
Now that they flutter through heaven
I commemorate them in song.

I PRAY FROM THE HEART A PSALTER . . .

I pray from the heart a psalter
with frayed edges and all the words missing I

see hover a long time now hover
and seeking to rest their feet how
shall I give them balm and heart
my psalter with mangled edges
is depleted and bare.

ME—I AM BUT ONE . . .

Me—I am but one. And there are thousands. How many
thousands and tens of thousands even and millions. And yet
I am but one myself and I have thousands and
tens of thousands and even millions who fall down together in the dust,
who mingle and thicken earth's crust and who raise
me slowly if not heavenwards
to bury me under themselves.

AFTER A THOUSAND YEARS . . .

After a thousand years, and I in my place. From it
I'm reluctant to move. After a thousand
I am in my place, that is my place. Also the thousand.
And what did they tell on the streets? And what did they seek? And
    what is it
that sensed back a thousand years
the moment of fear of a thousand years
the like of which has not been in a thousand years?

I WENT OUT INTO THAT WELCOME COLD . . .

I went out into that welcome cold of mine that's there
and remembered that I really didn't go out that they won't let me go out
and I to that cold of mine to myself must

Amir Gilbo'a   63

go out to my life which is now outside
in that welcome cold of mine that's there outside
just now

I DON'T WANT TO SEE BLACK BUT

I don't want to see black but
grey comes from every side and I know what
I don't want to know and I even don't bury
my head in the sand anymore here I must
stop if I don't want to say those
other things but what cries inside me
is

I PUT THE TIP OF THE PEN TO THE PAPER . . .

I put the tip of the pen to the paper like the barrel of a gun to the temple
now by pressing just once I shall shoot dead all the days and the nights.
My mistake. I won't shoot till this moment perhaps only this single
    moment
and those which follow it shall intermittently run on without me.
Whose consolation the slain that he is eternity?

ABBA KOVNER b. 1918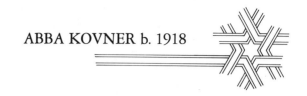

OBSERVATION ON A SOLITARY TREE

Turtledoves don't do it.
Only you tear through
returning again and again to the dark
moving the dead nest's lips for speech.

We need no longer the enlightening
lightning, where all is fated and all
comes about as it decrees. Even the worm in the apple
fulfills its mission by and by.

Unruffle your plumage! The apple tree
has only just unsheathed its daggers. Let it
face its burden without this iceberg
without your riddle.

THIS WAY, THIS WAY

You are the mother of my little ones lost some in the fire
some in the wood and some waiting for the gate
that does not open   you the mother of
my pretty little ones left unborn
for their sake I followed you
to the end of the fable
an unsown land
without an
end

NOTE APROPOS THE NEIGHBOR'S GARDEN

Spotless curtain. The garden has
both tender and fender. The cluster of roses
immaculately trimmed. The pampered pecan tree
will render in season. A bird

will return. To sing. The nuts too
someone will come and gather.
And the skin of the one sequestered inside
day after day peels further.

OBSERVATION ON A SMALL HARBOR
OUTSIDE THE MILITARY ZONE

At the tip of the old pier a boat trembled
battered as a beggar's hat under the face of a star.
The memory of day had not yet set. I don't know
where the two thought they were headed—
they entered it
in leaps. A lantern lit up:

Through its latticework
a poplar, fishbone-bare,
sifts a thin light. The bay water and all
that's beyond it and un-
explored
just then resembled a looking glass.
And he said to her: look,
look.

NOTE APROPOS A LIGHT BREEZE AND AN
ELDERLY COUPLE ON A BENCH, TOGETHER,
IN THE NATIONAL PARK AT RAMAT-GAN

The wind subsided
mellow. Tomorrow will continue fair.

March. April. May. In the last seven leaves
I discovered ten shades of green! I won't cry.
When have we seen stones change colors
like babes fresh from the bath—

Forty years
do you remember, how we flitted
indifferent each to each
running and flitting through rooms
emptied of one
and each.

SHLOMOH TAN'EE b. 1919

WE TWO

The palm of my hand touched but one spot
yet all the blood streamed by there on the double,
the whole body in the palm of my hand.

Just as my eyes, two tiny windows, see you
yet your beauty's delivered on the double
to all of me—and I'm on fire.

* * * * *

I was with you in a far-off land
where mortal voices were unheard,
where the chant of angels was unheard.

I was with you in the inner-inner city,
where heavy walls did not press us,
where the traffic noise did not trespass.

I was with you in the depth of the night.
We never sensed the wheel of fortune's turning,
nor the torchlight in the eyes of beasts.

And then we crossed the threshold of a room,
stepped on wet, sweet-scented dust
and did not remember what was, what was.

* * * * *

The messengers came hard pressed—rain drops.
The messengers came fleet footed—rays of dawn.
As though by chance, I wasn't home.

They always hound me, the sassy ones,
their breath—bone chilling—overtakes me.
Let's hope they never catch me.

END OF SUMMER

End of summer. Not spring's end, nor fall's.
Just end of summer. Melancholy. Lassitude. Void.
Apple scents trail the honey of the dates.
All's overripe, souring now, even the sweet.

The earth cowered helpless before the sun,
swooning, self-abnegating, aswirl.
End of summer. Melancholy. So much, so much already in the past.
Far too ripe are the body, the fruit, and the soul.

END SONG

Long glances heavy as lead.
The room is forgotten. You hint: "Well, bye."
In the heart that calls you it's already fall. But savage
is that fall—your royal summer's demise.

A smile. You shrink from my silent glances;
a smile—that veil over grieving tears.
Then I recall: There's a room around us.
Ancient and mute, ancient and dear.

Another hint. Heavy is the lead.
As a love declaration final and dying
I would toss you a kiss and a flower.
But the hand won't move. The lips hesitate.

BENJAMIN GALAI b. 1921

OF THE TRAVELERS THAT WON'T COME AGAIN

Not the dead shall praise you, Lord, today—
One by one impaled they drain.
And though it's the same to us—either way—
They are the travelers that won't come again.

Their name interred in darkness now—Lord God of Hosts!
One by one set out, did not arrive.
Slain the adolescent returns unto his dust
And through his mouth a profusion of roots drives.

Even our memory pales. Our sight's myopic.
The ones departed—send no whisper back.
What more can we do—than we have already?
What more, dear brother, in treason trapped?

Since not forever shall your sweetheart mourn you
And not forever look demurely down.
In your native village—the bells are tolling
As though you'd never left, and did not return.

And the soul of man? Does it live forever?
Who'll promise us—a charity or curse?
Rather a living dog than a dead lion,
For life is never proffered twice.

70

FROM THE NORTH POLE

We arrive,
under the light of a midnight sun,
at the open sea.
No more rocks, seagulls, kelp.
Only wind, wind.
The waters of the ends of the world, clear as glass.
The mass,
so long afloat underneath us,
stands still. Nor East, nor West.
Every step taken here—
forward,
back,
right,
or left—
if it won't pull us down into the abyss,
must now,
Dearest,
turn South.

THE DAYS OF SARAH

And the days
of Sarah were
one hundred years, and twenty, and seven.

And she died—
she vanished from the world on Mt. Hebron,
to the sound of the puttering feet of servants
whose very names she had forgotten.
All the family friends accompanied, shouldered her coffin
to its last resting place.
Its boards, it was said, were of the very thinnest,
ever so light.

And the days
of Sarah were

one hundred years, and twenty, and seven.
These were the days of Sarah.

Yet in truth her candle was snuffed many, many days before
she came to her last rest in the earth.
And the coffin in which she lay had been made all those years
out of the memory of split logs on another mountain,
on another mountain, in the Land of Moriah.

72   Benjamin Galai

THE ANGLERS

The line has been cast and all's preordained.
Where do they get this patience from
this peacefulness to wait
hour upon hour. Bit—no, didn't bite.
And according to what decree
do the fish approach the hooks or flee
that glittering moment in the air filled
with a layer of water pearls. Tears
in a sumptuous sun. And still
the outstretched arm.

And in the silvery fish, and in the captor's swing
the heart of the world is trembling.

ONE TINY BIRD

All his life he sought one tiny bird
to be at his side
either to his left or his right.
All his life he sought to be understood
among his own kind
yet would not dissemble
to lure that songbird
to his nest
and his best
to have it to his right

or his left
to sing on his behalf
free of fear and quite
unpossessed.

That it may just unintentionally stay
to empathize
without going out of its way.
And its voice in his
and its heart in his side.

All his life he sought one tiny bird.

THAT STREET OF MINE

Day before yesterday the street was a street.
Yesterday that same street had become a forest,
today that same street has become a beach
and a brother who's crossed the portals
to perish.

That's why I keep walking down that same street, down that same
    quarter,
just to gather from those familiar pavements
the standard farewells and surprise encounters
and to touch the events and rampant
gossip.

And I'm the blazer of trails, traverser of oceans
and I'm Columbus discovering land there.
And I'm Crusoe charmed by isolation
yet knowing his Friday is about to enter . . .

For actually my street is all the streets
and my eyes look through it like a net
to discover him from across the abyss—
and perhaps tomorrow I shall find the pluck
to acknowledge him gazing from the sidewalk,
to seize him by the coattail
and to quit . . .

74   Yekhi'el Mar

KHAYIM GURI b. 1922

HIS MOTHER

Following Deborah's song, long ago,
I heard the silence of Sisera's chariot (he being late),
Saw Sisera's mother watching from the window,
A woman with a streak of silver in her hair.

A spoil of dyed embroidery,
Two-toned embroidery for the neck of every spoiler, the maidens saw.
Meanwhile he lay in the tent as one asleep.
His hands quite empty.
On his chin traces of milk, butter, and gore.

The stillness remained unbroken by horses and chariots,
The maidens too fell silent one by one.
My silence had touched their silence.
Eventually the sun set.
Eventually the twilight petered out.

Forty years of peace in the land. Forty years
No horses galloped nor dead horsemen speared with glassy eyes.
But she died, shortly after her son's demise.

ODYSSEUS

And upon returning to his home town, he found a sea
And various fish and seaweed floating on the slow waves,
And a sun fainting on the heaven's rim.

Error breeds error, concluded Odysseus in his weary heart
And returned to the crossroads by the neighboring city,
To find a route to his home town untouched by water.

Worn wanderer as in a trance, and terribly homesick
Amid men who spoke a different Greek.
Those words he had packed as rations for his journey had long since
    perished.

At first he thought he had slept through many a day
And returned to men who were not astounded to see him
Nor stared agape.

He asked them with gestures and they tried to understand him
Across the distance.
The scarlet purpled and stalked the rim of those skies.

The elders rose and took the children who lingered about him in a ring
And dragged them away.
And light upon light gilded house upon house.

Dew came and descended on his head.
Wind came and kissed his lips.
Waters came and washed his feet like old Eurycleia.
And failed to see the scar and continued downhill as waters do.

THERE ONCE WAS A DOVE

There once was a dove
descended from above to my shoulder,
ever so light,
from the roofs of the city of charity and pity.

Together we kept our peace
an innocent hour with the wind in between.
I wanted to tell her:
Innocent, innocent dove,
You've found your resting place.

76   Khayim Guri

There once was a dove
landed on my shoulder,
white and warm.

Till my lips had touched her
and her plumage turned crimson red.

I FANCY THAT I'M STANDING GUARD . . .

I fancy that I'm standing guard over the battlements of a city
that perished long ago.

Those lights which flood me now
are testament to light extinguished years before.

I thread my path amid relics which time has abandoned;
move on.
Yet they survive, outside that striding time which crumbles in the
    clocks.

And they return to me, return to me to live more slowly
alongside ashtrays,
alongside cooling coffee cups.

I walk a lot, and hazard guesses
and relish the ensuing doubt.

But I stand guard over the battlements of a city that perished long ago.

YEHUDAH OFFEN b. 1922

LEAVES . . .

leaves
green as the sand's dream
swallowed a well

your shadow on grass
dew

on my lashes
the silk of your likeness

nothing is mine

AIR DRIPS FROM ROCK

Air drips from rock
light melts
clouds buckle
and sky explores

Ancient journey
in these stone tents
a crying
baby passed

Night inquires in the field
language of mutes
a stone bleeds echo
a flower retorts silence

INWARDS

Dim reading in a white book
by a window bolted
inwards
till midnight light

ponders its stars
a deserted night
and only the sun listens
in its dream

and just once
he moves suddenly out of himself
and a new shadow is born
in the recollecting eye

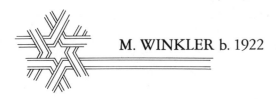

M. WINKLER b. 1922

THE SUN HELD IN TENDER HANDS

The sun held in tender hands
and hairs of light:
A sun that sinks into me
in the west.
I'm not at peace. The day
sheds transparent clouds
on my head,
it sheds the drawn-out years of a life
like fancied moments.
I'm not at peace—the evening hours all
toll in my heart,
the night hours all slowly inter
my mother.

BIRTHDAY

The flowers sent by the woman arrived too late.
And no one was in the apartment to receive them,
except two candles, and the wind blowing
the grey curtains.
On the floor—a drowsy black cat.
The messengers didn't know what to do
with the flowers, sent for the birthday
of someone
who had meanwhile departed, and they left them
outside the door.

CONCLUSION

I came to pay you a visit, but you were sad and I empty-handed,
the wine from the tumbler was spilled to the slaked ground
and I have no more; the flowers tore in the wind.
On the way I found a penny
and picked it up to bring you luck;
one must believe in superstitions
for it's hard to travel without castles in the air.
The sun is about to set,
soon it will consume all the horizons;
and after the fire the smoke will envelop them, always the smoke,
and after that—the void?
I came to pay you a visit, but you were sad and I empty-handed,
and I know—it's already too late to come
out of habit or pity alone,
and I know—it's already too late to live
out of habit or pity alone.

NIGHT AFTER NIGHT I COME TO WORSHIP

Night after night I come to worship the ripening light
like a butterfly falling into the lamp's net.
Night after night I come to obliterate myself
in your eyes, to soar like Icarus
beyond his heart.

Night after night the sea covers
my wings—burned to ashes—
morning after morning I return to my heart
with the newborn light.

AND SO THEY WITHERED

And so they withered
the trees outside the large casement of light—

M. Winkler   81

variegated from yellow to purple,
from brown to grey.
And so the trees withered, ever so slowly;
their personal failure passing
from tree to tree with the gait of an ancient king.
    Each spoke a different language,
      each dictated a different song.
And so the trees withered and lost their
leaves in the wind of a bustling city or desert—
    each tree according to its essence,
      outside the large casement of light.

AT THE ART EXHIBIT

The windmill on the riverbank
carries the dark clouds of Holland
on its shoulders.
Myself, am a child of the rocky desert;
in times of drought the nomad's thorns still sprout in me.
Only in dreams do I approach it
fighting;
only in dreams, when my sword breaks
across its wings,
is it milling my toughened grain into the white
flour of bread and cloud.

THE EVENING CLOSES OVER ME . . .

The evening closes over me like a grey seashell
abandoned on the beach, waves lapping at my heels
and my head curled since the happy days of childhood.
I used to be king in a Land of Dwarves and slave to a princess
in the Kingdom of the Soft-hearted Giants. I used to sit on the sill that
    was my house

82 M. Winkler

at twilight, wrapped in dreams; Mother wove the long fabrics
of thought to greet the sundry springtimes of her sons.
The night closes over me like a black seashell,
fish lapping at my flesh.

AHARON AMIR b. 1923

STONE

Matters have become very simple,
very vague,
very light,
unendurably easy . . .

The mist that immerses us in adulation
and the soft, the ticking twilight that licks our cheeks with its fingers
and the noiseless wind of peace, that rocks us gently, dependably . . .

No seeking the noonlight peal of yesteryear.
Pecking rather,
from the honey cake of now
the mustard-of-anxiety seeds,
the destructive, the explosive grain,
the alien pebble sequestered in the honeycomb,
the very slingshot of a future noon!

COCK

At dawn crowed the cock
and nearby tolled the bell
a tremor ripples your flesh
    —and rebounds

At dawn a cock crowed
a cock

and nearby a bell tolled
a bell
and your body would answer aloud
clamor aloud
    —quake

Love-time, a cock proclaimed
a cock
fingers fumbling on pillow
fumbling
and elbows extend to embrace
desiring chase
    —mute

Wind stalks through the corn
the corn
clouds in the realms of the sky
clouds
rivers go lapping their course
between hillocks kissing
    —their source

In the window the morning stands pat
stands pat
and on your bed the sun is again
laid out
but without the crow
    —of the cock

WHEN IT CAME TIME

When it came time to say good-bye
the saxophones blared from the jukeboxes
and the figures in the pit rocked their bodies
mechanically to the variegated rhythms of jazz

When it came time to say good-bye
a thousand drinks were downed at all the bars

and the bridge lights peered up from the river
the prostitutes slithered and sang along the outskirts
on the roads each car pursued its mate
and on the concrete pavements the paupers rested their bones

When it came time to say good-bye
we found ourselves very lonely in the big city
we found ourselves very innocent in the sophisticated city
it seemed to us suddenly that we were children
that even the world was a child of sorts
lacking words to put in our mouths
to let us express all of our essence
to let us share our whole effervescence
to let us truly say one to the other:
Good-bye

ODEON

And afterwards
by the tunnel entrance
soft and airy you
stood beside me
and by the cold, the
painful street light
your cheek trembled
and you lowered your eyes—

      (the signs pointed here and there
      and last trains pulled up close
      and the minutes sped on
      sped on
      toward the zero line—)

My kiss drowned
reeling, shame-faced
in the sudden flushing
of your cheek's white
and the light of your eyes

86   Aharon Amir

that shone from
under your lashes
dimmed all the
street lamps all at once—

And afterwards
words fell
one by one
like stifled:
"Good-bye"
"Thanks"
"See you":
and never, in all my life,
has there ever been
a tone so pure and ringing
to these battered words—
            (and the last of the trains turned to escape
            the signs didn't point to a single thing
            and the minutes fell dead
            fell dead
            fell dead
            on the finish line—)

EXIT FROM THE GARDEN OF DELIGHTS

The cycle's complete.
The garden turned silent, inert.
Your feet trudge through the leaves
and again you stand
alone
exactly where you had been.
At least that's what you can imagine in your mind
and tell your mind
apropos:
"Farewell, my soul.
What's been, has been
and is gone—

what's been has passed
and is gone—
the gallop of the rocking horse
the up and down of the swings
the Ferris wheel sway on high
the battle against the windmills
the scuttle with demons in the dark
slaughter of the dummies and dolls
the break-through, the strike, the flight
a sense of the action
perception of perspicacity
the assumed pomposity—
all that's over now.
Wiped clean."

The cycle's complete
and the game completed.
The stage lights are dimmed.
And the feet stand exactly where they stood before—
among fallen leaves.
And neither tempest
nor wind's there
and a strange hush caresses
these ears still ringing
from the tumult that was and is gone.
Across the expansive and peaceful square
evening throws itself headlong.
Somewhere a house awaits you.
Somewhere a meal is cooking for you.
Yet meanwhile
it's wise perhaps to grab a bite.
A couple of hot dogs, say.
A couple of hot dogs dressed
with mustard.

YEHUDAH AMIKHAI b. 1924

OF THE THREE OR FOUR IN THE ROOM

Of the three or four in the room
One always stands poised by the window.
Forced to watch the evil among weeds
The conflagrations on the hill.
And how men departing whole of limb
Are returned at nighttime like loose change to their homes.

Of the three or four in the room
One always stands poised by the window.
His dusky hair falls across his thoughts.
Speech is behind him.
And before him the vagrant voices without knapsack,
The hearts without provisions, the prophecies run dry
And those large stones which were returned
And left unopened like letters without
Either address or addressee.

FOR MY BIRTHDAY

Thirty-two times have I entered life
And each time pained my mother less,
The others less,
And me more.

Thirty-two times have I worn a world
That still won't fit.

It weighs on me,
Not like a coat, which takes its shape from mine,
Turned comfortable
And shoddy.

Thirty-two times have I checked the figures
Without finding the mistake,
Have begun the story
Without permission to conclude.

Thirty-two years have I carried with me my father's traits,
Though I've shed most along the road
So as to lighten the burden of my load.
In my mouth—straw. And I amazed,
And the beam between my eyes, which I'm unable to dislodge
Has begun to blossom in the spring—like trees.

And my deeds diminish
Bit by bit. Yet
The explications about them have grown, just as
The Talmud's made complex
And shrinks upon the page,
When commentaries
Besiege the text.

And now, after thirty-two rounds,
After these thirty-two years,
I'm parable still,
Unlikely to become its moral.
And I stand undisguised before the enemy's eyes
And yellowing maps in my hand,
Amid growing resistance and between towers,
And alone; with no recommendations
In this desert zone.

DEFOLIATED LEAVES

Defoliated leaves
Must wander.

Deviscerated blood
Is nonrecyclable;
It will dry in the roadway.
And even words must wean
Themselves from the lips,
Find new ones.
And the earth must purge itself
From history.
And the stones must sleep—
This one too
That slew Goliath, black shall sleep.

Yet I,
Like a shed
Turned makeshift temple,
Am now again abandoned.

And I,
Like the surveyors,
Must drive sharp hopes—
Black/white stakes—
Far into the wild terrain
Ahead.

MY FATHER

Four years my father fought their war,
With neither love nor hatred for his foes.
And yet I know that even there
He built me up daily for his few

Calm moments, those he snatched
Between the air raids and the smoke,
And put inside his tattered satchel
Beside his mother's dried-out cake.

And in his eyes he gathered the nameless dead,
A multitude of these he gathered in my name,
That in his glances I might recognize and love them

And not perish likewise in mortal dread . . .
He stuffed his eyes with them and yet he erred:
To all my battles am I alert.

LIKE TWO STONES AT THE BOTTOM OF A SLOPE . . .

Like two stones at the bottom of a slope we lie.
This far have we tumbled. Here we'll rest a while.

A year, or two or more we'll stall
watching summers abdicate to fall.

Our pocked bodies go about
sensing the sun and shadow of the clouds.

And under us in summer spring's soil
palpitating still and still moist.

Teeming black life and yet unbroken—
and ours alone, and quite unknown.

BOTH OF US TOGETHER AND EACH APART

"Both together and each apart," clause from a lease.

Sweetheart, another summer's gone
And my father never came to the Luna Park.
And the swings swing on and on.
Both of us together and each apart.

The sea's horizon mislays its ships,
Difficult now not to lose one's grip.
Behind the mountain the warriors tarried.
And what a craving we have to be pitied.
Both of us together and each apart.

There's a moon that saws the clouds in twain—

92   Yehudah Amikhai

Come let us go on a loving campaign.
Only we two in a duel of love.
Possibly everything may still be resolved.
Both of us together and each apart.

My love has transformed me, it would seem
Like a salt-water sea to the sweet drops of rain;
Am slowly brought to you and collapse.
Receive me. We have no guardian angel's lap.
For both of us are together. Each is apart.

THE CLOUDS ARE THE FIRST FATALITIES

The clouds are the first fatalities,
the stones at the edge of the river bed
are the last.
How much time's elapsed between them
we've stubbornly denied, said nothing of. But
the earth must say it all
in the probe of rain and sun, all
that she knows, grass, cyclamens,
sundry flowers; and the grass will wither and weeds climb.

Easy for us to have loved had we cared to,
when the beloved's face opens wide as wings
and death is folded like planes
in the boat that carries them. Easy to have loved,
and I don't know whether we'll have another chance.
The equilibrium would be disrupted; the waters unevenly parted,
the clock stumble like pupils who memorized and forgot,
and into the history displayed in museums
the terrible heat will burst and when the guards
will no longer be able to defend the heavy doors
the barriers will vanish.

Only Death demands punctuality from us;
His black barriers are impassable,
and it remains for us to color in the empty

spaces, like children in a picture book
under the eyes of a supervising God.

And we assumed that He was cruel,
because of His unkempt hair.
And all the while judgment will be passed
and machine guns of verdicts and rulings
shoot out in direct fire and hit dogs,
hit my hand, and little Ruthy and those too
whose number was not yet up,
and all by chance. As in building a house when suddenly
one discovers broken walls and shards: an ancient
city unpeels and the sky forgets and retreats
behind the stars that remained to cover its retreat.

Or, for example, when my father died
and they carried him from his place and his place remained empty
as a manhole in mid-road, when an iron cover
is lifted, and God decked out in blue overalls
descended there to make repairs, and the candle on
the floor like a light to warn pedestrians
and the last words adjusted
slowly to being last
underneath the hope of night's ceiling—
perhaps then was the time
to love and stay on.

But now time's turned docile and dim
in our hands like a port against the sides of ships
that have anchored there too long;
likewise justifications of tardiness or
forgetfulness won't help us.
The heavens forget.
And we are like the stalks of flowers in a vase.
Bound at bottom in the dark,
and stifled. And above, beyond the vessel's rim
are skies of open flowers, and each has its own
flower, yet who of us knows it below,
in the dark, one alongside the other. And near death.

94 Yehudah Amikhai

THE DIAMETER OF THE BOMB
WAS THIRTY CENTIMETERS

The diameter of the bomb was thirty centimeters
and the diameter of its hitting range about seven meters
and within it four dead and eleven wounded.
And around these, in a wider circle
of pain and time, are scattered two hospitals
and one cemetery. But the young
woman, who was buried in the place from which
she came, at a distance of over one hundred kilometers,
enlarges the circle very much,
and the lonely man who weeps over her death
at the ends of one of the overseas countries
includes the entire world in that circle.
And I won't even mention the cry of the orphans
which reaches the throne of God
and from there onward making
the circle endless and godless.

THE OLD ICE FACTORY IN PETAKH TIKVA

The old ice factory in Petakh Tikva,
a wooden tower whose boards rot in darkness.
In my childhood crying had its home there.
I remember the tears
dropping from board to board,
to allay the raging summer
and to make ice below
glide out of a deep hole.

And behind the dusky cypresses, the talk
commenced right off: "One lives
only once."

I didn't understand then,
and now that I do, it's too late.

Yehudah Amikhai 95

The cypresses are still standing there
but the dropping water continues elsewhere.

EARLY IN THE MORNING YOU LEAN . . .

Early in the morning you lean on the wall of an old house,
powerful crutch. Then you hop lightly
aboard the bus with the other hoppers.

In these sacred sandals daily
you go to work at the office,
in these garments of love, to widen and tighten.

What is it protects you? Stockings, very
sheer, up to your navel.

What holds up the old house?
Memory holds it up. Till you come
again to lean on it the next morning.

FOR MY BELOVED, COMBING HER HAIR . . .

For my beloved, combing her hair without mirror across from me,
a song: You've washed your hair with shampoo,
an entire pine forest homesick on your head.

Internal and external silence
have like inert copper plated your face between them.

The pillow on your bed will be your stand-by brain
crumpled under your head for remembering and dreaming.

Under us the earth trembles, Beloved.
We'll lie clasped together, a double lock.

96   Yehudah Amikhai

THE PEOPLE ON THIS BEACH WILL NEVER

The people on this beach will never
again sink the soles of their feet
in the traces they left in passing.

It is a tearful truth,
but sometimes it cries from joy
that the world is large and one does not need to return
in it. It all goes under one sky.

Towards evening I saw a tanned
lifeguard go down on a blonde he rescued
to resuscitate her with his mouth, like lovers.

Yehudah Amikhai   97

ANADAD ELDAN b. 1924

FOAM BLANCHES

You approach sleep like voices trying to reach
to break through into
the storm in the waves of your body
foam blanches as far as the shore
retreating to all the corners of the expanse
of your tiny sea
in this whiteness many ships
perish.
Yet your eyes are sealed.

THE CANDLE OF BRIEF TIMES

Those whose time
resembles an hourglass
sensibility drains from them
in uniform rhythm
combustible. Always the paupers.
The candle of brief times.
Their sensibility drains in a uniform stream
and when they recall
its yellowish tint their sorrow grows,
their body hastens to become a drawn bow,
to dispatch an arrow
and from their stricken head
sunset skies pour.
They turn yellow between their fingers.

98

BETWEEN THE WHITE STONE CANYONS

Between the white stone canyons
once the cries become enfeebled
bounding from wall to wall
and you are locked amid the cliffs
with heaven for canopy
you open to the stillness
which is a dialogue
between nobler silence
and baser silence
your eyes sail to the summit
and float
your neck extended towards your Father.

AT YOUR NAKED BACK

At your naked back naked earth
you failed to sever the dark
from it, and the light dove right back
in the water. And over you the mountain you wished
would separate the waters.
Let its stony shoulders bear the sky
over you. Two stones heavy to the touch.
I plucked leaves, parched dry in summer
they kiss the moisture in your eyes that fill
with weariness and memories; silently then you lit up—
to listen to those naïves, the domestic grasses
that will cushion your sleep.

TSFRIRAH GAR b. 1924

AFTER THE GUESTS DEPARTED

What tribute have we failed to pay?
What did we forget to deliver?
The emptiness
that remained after the guests departed—
as though they took
with them the booty
and left us deep in debt.

FIRST RAIN

The downpour fills the heavens
with crooked rulers
that divide the winds of heaven
into grey and narrow strips
I can't put my finger on that sorry spot
on the window behind which yesterday only
the sun had burned.

ONLY STATUES DON'T SHY AWAY

Chips fly off around them
fragments that were cast about.

Yet still the stone retains
a form, a hidden motion
which the chisel could not overcome.

Without the bat of an eye
or signal or whisper.
Yet he who closes his eyes
and he who stops his ears shall find it.
Affecting and touching as a handshake.

SEEING THE LIGHT

The worm, at long last, must find
the other side of the radish
and see the light.

The burrowing one had
no destination.
It did not dig for freedom,
only toiled to fill its stomach.
Yet from that bitter moment,
seek out
for itself it will—
crawling on its belly—
another root,
and whole.

TIN TOYS

To the tin toys there was
a motion particular,
precise.
One had to wind them,
so they could begin to move like us—
almost.

Enthusiastically beat the drum.
A key (pole and hole underneath)
was the secret behind the success.
The hand took hold and activated with ease.
We had the pleasure
to move,
induce and give life.
To egg on and whet their appetite to move.
Sometimes we'd extract the key,
experimentally,
from their utter
docility;
and be startled as a wild start still left
and breaking free
in the secret spring we forgot about
sprang on us
of a sudden.

GROWN OLD AND FULL OF YEARS

Grown old
and full of years
he hunches over and
sets down letter upon letter
carefully laid out,
dispatches them
black as insects and beasts
across the
insatiable page.

He writes
of seven mills
(that will not know a wind),
and waterfalls whose façades have fallen;
of banks grown waste
and fishes, swept away,

come—spread out like silver—
to die along the bank.

A boat
    sails down
        and down
to the river's mouth
        to a cold horizon
that will cover it
        in a little while
it will be gone.

SALT STATUES

Terror sculpted
and petrified us.
Where it found us—
us, who turned round
to learn more
of a flood to come
and wipe clean the face of the earth.
The destruction before the flood
annihilated
and laid bare the salt-bitten
empty expanses . . . fields of white statues.

Utter chaos, stone from stone
a deep furrow unlodged
the city
the end of all Flesh and Will!
The cloven earth
all scars
gapes with startled mouths.
Ruined salt sentries
that petrified at the sight.

A SPOT ON THE SUN

That circle
when full
is blinding.
To everyone.

Suns light up,
pursue,
anyone who looks—
too long.

Today they said
the circle's broken.
And the sun eclipsed.
A dark spot on the sun
covers it.

We'll steal another
look—
then look away.
For a long moment,
against scalding
eyelids
we retain
the margins of the sun
which burn
like white-hot iron
from under a cloud,
before it will sink and be gone.

IN THE HOUSE AT MIDNIGHT

In the house at midnight, in full light, we whisper;
but since no one's asleep
there's no one to wake.
Against the wall leans the black clock
its face, with two exclamation marks, opaque.

We're careful not to bump into things,
and move in the lamplight's circle
as though caught in alien territory,
surrounded by an invisible wall.

Like diligent thieves (gloved) we dare to covet
the rosy apple
smiling from the bowl,
and the fresh drink cavorting in the bottle,
and the books conspiring on the shelf.

We closet ourselves inside the circle of light,
sink cautiously into the creaking armchair.
Uncomfortable . . . from one crack or another
we're being watched unsparingly.

As subtenants all these years
it's strange we've never bumped into him;
like butterflies we hover.
And when the clock suddenly sings out
we scatter all at once, so as not to be caught
by the hand of the Dark.

TUVIA RÜBNER b. 1924

SUNFLOWER

Wheel of light without beginning,
Wheel of light without an end,
Revolving sword of holy fire,
Angels' wings in saraband
Round a dim, a dying pupil,
Round a dark and muted heart.

SPRING IN THE LAND

Gigantic flowers, as though
They were made for dwelling,
Transparent clouds in the blue
Like heart's mellowing.

Butterflies sprouting, as though
They had never yet seen the light,
My flesh against yours, as though
My blood with yours unite.

Licking flames of birds, as though
Heaven were at last content,
Blossoms of bliss, as though
Spring were in the land.

THE FIRE THAT IN THE STONE

Even in sleep I see you
and my terror flows towards bliss
like me—who flow into your palm.

As leans the rainbow on the cloud,
the wind upon the torso of the trees,
head upon shoulder—so you on me may lean.

And settled in your heart, as in the ark,
I've crossed alive that nightmare lake.

Purged clean of all, inhabit me from hereon
as I shall inhabit my bones.

As in the stone shall loiter fire,
as in the "no" reside the "yes"

Your voice with love respire.
United we in intellect.

MY FATHER

That every night my father
shone like the window in the ark.

That every night I was like a shadow
clinging to the wings of his light.

Tonight my father sweeps over me
as over a candle the dark.

IN THE EMPTY STREET EVERY SHUTTER IS BOLTED

In the empty street every shutter is bolted.
Where did I come from? and where

am I going? The flanks
of the houses are grey in the scorching sun. Here's not

Where my house is. This isn't my street. My house
isn't here, the scorching sun
underfoot. No one's with me,
in all the street no man can give

Me an answer, one redeeming word . . .
—And suddenly the lurching car,
masked faces . . . a scream . . . and a pointed arm . . .
My God, my God, open a door for me!

LULLABY

The leopard, nocturnal, with eyes infernal,
In the dark, in the dark, how his fangs sparkle,
His claw fine as a blade;
Sleep tight, my child, in the wood.

Should you sleep, should you slumber, may God grant
You won't see your mother, in a pail decant
The lavender eyes of the light,
To allay the thirst of the maker of night.

Close your eyes now and sleep,
In the heavens a star weeps,
A star on your mother's brow.
In vain my leopard lies low
In the dark, in the dark, in the wood,
In the dream at your throat like a blade.

BEN-ZION TOMER b. 1928

COPY
from Song Sequence

My father engraved his life in stone.
I on wind.
My father appointed his house in warm brown tones, and in concrete
I in shades of sleet and feather paraphernalia lighter than wind.

My father breathed with his Lord,
I with the hawk—
My father sprang from the neighborhood,
I not even from home.

My father kept silent; his heart throbbed.
I throb. My heart keeps silent.

My father's already dead. Small temple his due—a stone.
I live still, and my temples are in the wind.
What shall remain, when like chaff I'm blown?
My son won't inscribe on a tablet my name.

HEARTFELT PITY
from Song Sequence

With dagger drawn I pass through the shop of your lovely toys.
I murder the multicolored bubbles before your eyes,
Behead the wooden dolls,
Set them on fire.
There's no magic, I say to you, like reality.

109

Perplexed.
Silent.
You regard me with the eye of a dead fish.
Alien to my pity,
Heartfelt pity.

PHANTOMS

I closed my eyes:
Those same faint voices,
stalking softly,
in their socks.

Phantoms.
Always circumventing the orbits of the sun
as I circumvent a dead mouse on the road.
They don't say a word.

At night they come,
stealing through memory's lattice.
Always always that carful of silence
which emptied of its children as though of coal.
Their warm breath.
The abandoned
Raggedy-Ann.
In the corner—
a small paper ship.
Buttons.
Thread.
Angels with faces the color of wax.
Now then they're rising. Have risen. Are gone.
Only in my neck is their eye still lodged.

DON QUIXOTE

Weary of dreams and forays
Don Quixote woke up that day
and looked in the glass:
His head with Sancho Panza's was interchanged.
A grey donkey stood at the doorstep. He mounted it.
His long legs dragged limply across the earth.
He rode. And rode. The vast distance a kingdom of silence and sun
in his flesh like a vulture's claws. Thorns pricked his eyes.
    He closed them slowly
towards the dream. For the first time in years a blank sleep
overcame him. No echo. No voice. Drowsing
he rode. In the light of an open window he saw Dulcenea's face
and covered his own. The sun set. Evening fell.
Shadows attacked him with the flashing of spears.
An old fire kindled his heart, he longed to storm the windmills,
but Sancho's head arrested him at once:
"Calm down, my friend, at ease!"
The smell of the forage spurred the donkey on. Slowly his hand let the
    whip drop.
They rode in silence: the head of Sancho and the heart of Don Quixote.

AVNER TRAININ b. 1928

SUNBEAMS

Don't let the sun go out!
Take paper, smiles and brotherhood
And fashion suns *en masse*—
Like cookies, cut out with a glass.

Make it a circle
And lines emanating from it
(They'll cry: Deceit! Deceit!):
Two lines like arms
Spread, with a fistful of seed;
Two lines like legs
Spelling love to the land,
And add on many more—
Don't stint!
As many as you need to span
Outward from you to other men.

CAT IN THE DOVECOT

Climbed up, devoured. In her beak
She shall bear nothing more.
Bring back no message to the ark.

Was done and then in peace
Slid down upon his paws—
Upholstered blades.

Found himself a resting place
And picked the bones.

Trickle.
Mere trickle.
There shall be no more flood.

ANCIENT SONG

All's been said,
all's been sung.
It would hardly be wrong
to say nothing.
Yet the silence has a song
that must be undone.
That's why the bird chattered—
that song is shattered—
atop a tree's skeleton
bleak in this world's room.

All has been sketched,
all has been etched,
and if I were to do it right
this page'd be white.
Yet there's an outline to Nothing
that requires clothing;
that's why the fall designed—
ancient is that line—
the skeleton of that tree
on which the bird chattered—
ancient is that song—
atop this world's room.

PINKHAS SADEH b. 1929

THE ANGEL

Death rides a horse in the sky.
Lightly and splendidly it rides across the blue, in silence.
Death rides a horse in the sky, and it has the face of a girl.
The color of her eyes is like amber. Her feet are lily-white.
She carries a sword carved from the body of the sun, a sword
held over the four ends of the earth.
A sword over Damascus and Amon, a sword held over Jerusalem.
A sword over the innocent and the wise, lender and borrower, lover
and celibate alike.
Death rides a horse in the sky.
On the ground a poet sits and scribbles her face on the water.
The water thunders in fog and foam, and he scribbles her face on the
water.
In the woods the monkeys frolic, dogs bark, kingdoms fall, prophets
dream their god; some women have been abandoned, others are
beloved.
And many buy and sell and build houses,
and they have the names of the living but are really dead.
This world is beyond salvation.
Death rides a horse in the sky, across the blue in silence.
Its face is that of a girl, her feet white as lilies.
The color of her eyes is like amber. She smiles.
At her feet crocodile and pestilence lie, blood and the hemlock cup,
at her feet lament and terror and the abyss without end,
but her feet are lily-white and her face is a maiden's.

114

Over woods, flowers, and grass, over the all-embracing sea,
over the rivers of Damascus and Amon, over the mountains of
Jerusalem and Sinai,
Death rides a horse in the sky.

DAN PAGIS b. 1930

THE JOURNEY

He who dreads arrival and speeds in the night
between iron bridges that draw apart
and whose wire-strung skies interchange in the window—

He who speeds in the night and whose blood ticks away
between glowing numerals and slackens when near arrival—
shall find between lights splashed in his face, far away

An unmoving star in an uncalculated space
in an orbit that crosses between them
neither at the appointed hour nor right now

Nor from any world to any world.
Singly they both stand
in the invisible light.

BROTHERS

1

Abel was fair and woolly
and quasi modest
like the least of his gentle lambs,
curly as the smoke of the offering he sent
before the Lord his Master.
Cain was direct: like a knife.

2

Cain ponders. His large palm gropes
inside the slaughtered throat before him:
Where does that silence break from?

3

Abel remains in the field. Cain remains Cain. And because
he is sentenced to wander, he wanders diligently. Exchanges
each morning horizon for horizon. One day he discovers:
The earth has deceived him over the years. It moved, but
he, Cain, was walking in place. He stomped, stepped, ran,
on only a single spot of dust, precisely the size of his sandals.

4

On a merciful night he chances upon
a fine haystack.
He sinks down, is swallowed up, rests.
Hush, Cain's asleep.
Happy, he dreams that he is Abel.

5

Don't be afraid, don't be afraid.
It has already been decreed that he who would kill you
shall be punished sevenfold.
Your brother Abel protects you from all harm.

AUTOBIOGRAPHY

I died at the first blow and was buried
in the rocky ground.
The raven showed my parents
what to do with me.

My family's respected, not least on my account.
My brother invented murder,
my parents lament,
I silence.

Dan Pagis   117

Then those well-remembered events came to pass.
Our inventions were perfected. One thing led to another,
edicts were published. Some killed in their own fashion,
some wept in their own fashion.

I won't mention names
out of consideration for the reader,
for at first the details may horrify,
but in the end they weary:
You may die once, twice, even sevenfold,
but you can't die ten thousand times.
I can.
My underground cells reach everywhere.

When Cain began to propagate on the face of the earth
I began propagating in the belly of the earth,
and have long since overpowered him.
His legions desert him and join me,
and even that is only half a revenge.

A MOMENT AT THE LOUVRE

I'm rushing to an important meeting:
Inside his glass case expects me
(I am already late) the skillful scribe of the Pharaoh.
Seated cross-legged,
all intent
he regards me with white eyes.
What shall I dictate to him?

Chance visitors pause for a moment,
are reflected in the pane, are effaced.

So it's the two of us.
His knees regard me patiently.
So what?
He's burnt clay,

I'm clay that hardens by-and-by.
What can I bequeath him?

Immobile almost he observes
my silence.
He inscribes it
on a blank tablet.

I glance at my watch, and by-and-by am effaced
from the pane, from his sight.
He didn't notice that I'd already been.
He expects me.
I'm already late.

POINT OF ORIGIN

Hidden in the library at dusk
I wait, not quite lonely yet.
A massive walnut cabinet opens the night for me.
The grandfather clock, tired sentry,
slackens its steps.

From where? In Grandfather's typewriter,
an Underwood model from days gone by,
thousands of alphabets await.
What is the message?

I think not all's in doubt,
I trail the moment, that it shouldn't give me the slip.
My arms are somewhat thin.
I am nine years old.

Outside the door begins
the intergalactic space for which I'm already prepared.
Weight drains from me like colors at sunset.
I fly very fast, till I'm motionless,
and leave behind me
the transparent trail of the past.

Dan Pagis   119

HIDE AND SEEK

In the backyard of the world
we played, he and I,
I covered my eyes, and he hid:
One two three,
not in front, not behind,
not inside me.

Since then I've been searching
so many years.
So what if I don't find you?
Come out already, out,
you can see that I've given up.

IMPROMPTU HEART

Impromptu heart, acrobat without rope
or respite, how soon?
Below stir the horses of the brightly lit arena,
the plumes on their heads bounce in greeting.
Already in syncopated rhythm
the sadly wailing tuba mourns you
and the double-bass, that sentimental fogy.
Toward your fall far below
in the pit the drum
tightens.

But this blue space,
but this free fall,
but this poignant joy, oh heart.

THE ELEPHANT

The elephant, ancient general, scarred,
skin of an elephant, patience:

On the columns of his legs stands a worldful of
belly. But
that is his strength, that he overcomes himself from within:
At the crucial moment,
with cotton-wool caution,
with a love independent of the material,
he steps on sixteen marvellously precise wrist-watches,
puts four to each foot,
and glides on them with ease as though on skates
right out of his elephantine lot.

ARMCHAIRS

The slowest animals are
the soft leather armchairs with giant ears,
in the parlor corner.
They multiply
in the shade of a philodendron pot
or dusky rubber-plant.
And though they are content to live
more slowly than elephants,
they continually embark
on a secret safari without end.

FOSSILS

Those creatures that live forever, the fossils,
are stubborn all beyond compare.
The royal arch-fly fossilized in amber
despises time and catches with a thousand eyes
its noon-sleep in the sun.
The arch-conch is an ear refusing to listen.
The arch-fish even renounced itself,
and left only the impress of its bones in the rock.

The ultimate creation among fossils
is the Venus de Milo, that eternal denier whose
arms are air.

BALLOONS

Party balloons fondle each other
amid paper snakes,
and mildly accept
the limit, the ceiling of the hall.
Ready for any signal,
careful to obey each breeze.
Yet even these unassuming ones
must meet their end.
Suddenly their soul flies off
in a startled whistle,
or their soul explodes
with a single snap.
Later the rubber bodies wear out
at the edge of a soiled carpet
and the souls wander lost
in limbo, roughly level with your nose.

TWO-LEGS

Two-Legs is the queerest of creatures:
Bodily he is related
to the other predatory animals, yet he alone
cooks animals, seasons animals,
he alone wears animals, even on his feet.
He alone thinks
that he's an alien in the world, he alone protests
against his lot, he alone laughs,
and stranger yet, he alone

voluntarily rides a motorcycle.
He has twenty fingers,
two ears,
one hundred hearts.

MOSHEH DOR b. 1932

SAFETY PIN

We have no visions
And no stars, and no dawn and no field of bronze.
We fondle fate, or if we do petition—
Why, in statistical columns.

                                        Checking the office clock,
We file away the time
And fasten with a safety pin
Questionnaires to love, to ruin, to seizures, and to triumph.
From the morning to the evening papers
We climb the dim ladders of carbon sheets,
Chew sandwiches and peek
Down the new girl's bosom—be she plump or trim.
We have no rider-sun, we have no lightning-flower,
We have no ship of death,
No wailing of the sea—
But we have a party ledger, it only
Will stand by us and is for ever and ever.
We pay our taxes,
We sleep with our wives,
And fornicate only with our eyes;
We attend the second showing, sit in the café,
And when the director passes, we rise;
And sometimes we reflect that death's not bad, not far away,
Then hurry to push it beyond the files of our eyes.

AT A LOSS

I am at a loss on this very street
whose houses and gardens are arranged coffee-table neat
yet my hand is in my son's hand and his glance is anchored
      in my face.
That his boat may not budge I pretend to bravery and manners.
Even as the demon's wing beats at my back
and the warm air glides in waves across my trembling cheeks
I go on smiling (my Lord, naked I stand before You
and vast is the night all about)
and bend over my son:
"Look, a bird! Look, a cat!"
I am at a loss on this very street.

THERE'S A CERTAIN DIFFERENCE IN THE AIR

There's a certain difference in the air.
Someone's been dropped from the census
to death.
At the foot of the mountains angels breathe
in the bosom of the mist and appear
from the valley of the shadow of death.
Thank you, my Lord, for the guidance
of love, for the dream and the instant
of bliss.
Is the sun still there? Explain what "sun" is!
In the tresses of the earth twinkles the dew or maybe
the anointing oil.

Mosheh Dor   125

ELI NETSER b. 1933

THESE COLORS THIS TUNE

These colors. This tune. These
hands
this soft light. The colors. The tune.
Even the vine sprouted green flowers. Even
I listened to the voices. Footsteps died out
and someone came. This tune.
Once upon a time I'd heard it, yes. The colors, too. Even
the hand with its long fingers. Where have I seen it
   seen it

MY BEST CLOTHES

I take my old clothes out of the cupboard and deck
my body with them. My old clothes are really my best.
They always bear the scent of time, the faded color of oblivion
and a single wrinkle of memory. Perhaps that's why I don't like
new clothes that have glamour and chic but not
the touch of your fingers and that one hair shed when
you leaned with your head on my shoulder. Oh, how many new
clothes have I worn in my life! None among them can equal
the shirt frazzled from age you wiped your tears with.
Or the battered shoes in which I once stood, on a rainy night,
under your window. I am wearing old clothes which
are really my best and I notice that a new button gleams
in the place of another once lost in your bed. And I weep.

126

THIS FUGITIVE BEAUTY

If I could fetch you all the poets,
all the sculptors, all the architects of the dazzling
forms and bridges arching from here to there.
If I could fetch you all the painters with
their magic palettes, and all the other artists,
all of them. Wailing wailing soundlessly. Depleted like the hour-
glass
is this fugitive beauty.
At least then put
your hand in-
to mine.

LOOKING AT A CHAGALL PAINTING

Floating over the roofs and amid clouds, the violin in his hand.
He has no place on the topsy-turvy earth and on the hard
cobblestones. On the solid earth of the heavens and the paths
of clouds, strewn with the fallen leaves of stars, he carries his eternal
rucksack. The wind plays a soft Jewish medley on the
strings of his violin. His beard points the way back down.
Ultimately he will return from his wanderings, rest and then soar again
that he may set our dreams afloat.

THE MORE

Indeed profound. The more sacred. The more inscrutable.
The more. Only once again. If it were only given once again.
Now one puts it differently. One always puts
it differently. The more steady. Only once again.
Profound indeed. To charm as though with amulets.
Kingdoms fell. Towns turned to ashes
and time has ground the bones of heroes to powder.
Only the fables. The profound indeed
the more nonverbal, the more featureless.

Eli Netser   127

The song. The more melody.
One always puts it differently,
the names of one's loves change.
To beware of the sin of speech.
The painful indeed.
If I could sing or play this moment of my life
I would scorn the two thousand years of the olive.

STAR-SOWN

And already morning. The sun kisses the sown field
yet you are still lusting with a hunger gone wild. I am
beguiled, for sometimes it seems that as a lover I'm reviled
perhaps because I want to kiss everything like
the wind. Perhaps because I want to inhale all
the fragrance even if my mouth agape is terror-filled
and the world between my eyes is sprawled both lovely and
despoiled. And again I am beguiled—perhaps it is
that hunger gone wild. Perhaps this morning and you. Even now
the night under my eyelids is a star-sown field.

NIGHT WALK

And so we went
the Night and Federico and I
we divided the moon slice for slice
and aired our sorrows in song.
The Night said Wind
Federico said Guitar
and I Silence.
Then we knocked on the windows
and the whole town rose to its dream.
For each we sliced a slice of moon.
Then Federico wept a solitary song

until the guitar strings snapped
and again we wandered over the naked earth
and loved her up till insensate.

The Night went after the moon.
Federico in the blood of his song
and I alone remained to tell.

ALMOND BLOSSOMS

White-of-blossoms almond in the rain—
Young girl weeping on her wedding eve.

That fragrant, that heaving plain—
a pregnant woman her time arrived.

A puddle reflecting the light of the moon.
A tear of joy in your tiny palm.

*

Though the almond in its blossoms dressed
its tears the earth would not repress.

The rooftops from every road
whispered their blossom applause.

And when the tree of your body shed its gown
all of my fingers burst into song.

Eli Netser   129

DAVID AVIDAN b. 1934

CRADLE SONG

Come here, little girl, come here,
into sleep disappear,
come to me in the soft dusk,
that the angel of death take both of us.
Come here, come here, my precious pearl,
come here, come here, my melancholy girl,
approach alone the man who died,
and become good friends indeed.
Come here, come here, wonder-girl,
hurry to the pleasure-isle,
hurry to that strange inferno
even good Uncle Dante didn't know.
And now come here, come here, big girl,
come here, come here, my pitiful pearl,
and ride a sleigh in the failing light
into the dark—cold and desolate.
And therefore get up, get up, feeble girl,
get up and leave, a woman,
get up and travel the years until
both of us be done and undone.

SLEEP, LEOPARD, SLEEP

He has time.
He is danger-destined-to-come.
He is destined to come

to the other woods.
Yet meanwhile nightmares master him,
and he turns in his sleep,
left and right,
forward and back,
upwards and down.
Suddenly a certain prospect pops up, for the ancient elephants, no less.
They recall worse days than these.
They surround him like a flock of midwives
and trumpet lullabies for him,
tunes to disarm him.
What will happen if the leopard wakens in the middle of
the penultimate dream?
What will happen if I myself don't appear in his dream
nor he in mine
or in his?

DOMINATION AS ANOTHER FORM OF WEAKNESS

Hopeless, this weakness of mine,
it refuses to live, this weakness in me.
From her viewpoint it's a crime
to be or not to be
both in the Shakespearean sense
and in the others equally.

Anyway she's already dying
whenever she begins to mellow
and therefore of course not relying
at crucial moments on herself.
Since I really can't help
her, I'm for myself as ever.

PERSONAL PROBLEMS

My love was so overwhelming it would not bear the telling.
It would not bear the telling, it was so overwhelming.

David Avidan   131

My love was so overwhelming.
Till a time came when I could tell you.
I could tell you because I loved you.
Because I loved you.
The trees budded their greenery and the sun's face turned black.
And the more I loved you the blacker it got.
Like a certain species of leopard. Remote, poised for attack.
(Really, it had the leopard's spots.)
And then we came to town.
A lily acknowledged me.
And woke me in the morning.
But I loved you nevertheless.
The final light dawned and removed all doubt and left
only the movie house, white and glowing in the sun.
And he who still has something to hide
let him keep out of the sun.
And let him who loves not go to town.

THE STREETS AT THEIR LEISURE RISE

The loveliest of streets will come to an end by and by.
And the peace, opaque and hard, will be sliced like a loaf lengthwise.
And the morning, moist, from one stroke of lightning, its own, will
    carbonize.

People will gasp for breath as at the end of an old-fashioned ride.
The concrete-belt of this city is fastened. Fastened tight.
The massive walls comprehend something and topple and are quiet.

And outside an absolute sunlight descends on the city that dies.
On such a day that no baby is born in any house is no surprise,
nor is there a single demise. And indeed the streets at their leisure rise.

Like a magic carpet the streets rise towards the white light.
And the toppled walls are again somehow tall (citizens are wise).
And the city has neither beginning nor end. And all entrance is denied.

And your hands sing against the wall, like the murmur of green moss.

132   David Avidan

And your eyes bloom like rhinestones on the lightning's throat.
Only your mouth whistles. And in the profound light only your tired
    head floats.

THE SPOT REMAINED ON THE WALL

Some tried to scratch the spot off the wall.
But the spot was much too dark (or on the contrary—too light).
Either way—the spot remained on the wall.

And I sent for the painter to cover the wall with green.
But the spot was much too light.
And I hired a plasterer, to plaster the wall white.
But the spot was much too dark.
Either way—the spot remained on the wall.

And I took a kitchen knife and tried to peel the spot off the wall.
And the knife was painfully sharp.
It was whetted only yesterday.
Andyet.
And I clutched an axe and beat on the wall, but stopped in time.
I donow why suddenly it occurred to me
that the wall mightopple, andyet the spot remain.
Either way—the spot remained on the wall.

And when they stood me against the wall, I asked to stand real close.
And I covered it with my broad chest (who knows: maybe).
And when they peppered my back, much blood spouted but only
    alongside.
Fire.

And I believed so much that the blood would cover the spot.
A second barrage of fire.
And I believed so much that the blood would cover the spot.
Either way—the spot remained on the wall.

ITAMAR YA'OZ-KEST b. 1934

APPLES

Apples
the color of cold
on the waiting man's table.

A forgotten landscape
clad in autumn's cloak
raps:

Time to stand
in the doorway of
yourself.

YONDER

Morning's roof
churns
the deep blue of the yonder.

A chip
of lake.

Birds settle
on the roof's edge
to wash the dark
from their faces.

For how long
is this one
hour of morning mine?

ON THE RIVER LOOKOUT

On the river lookout a goldfinch screamed
and the lily of the night opened a frightened eye—
a soldier the color of earth
inhaled the autumn wind
and crossed his city's threshold.
He saw the light from the windows drip yellow in the river
like wine on the familial table. He approached
bowing low to the years
kissing his loved ones' mouths in the water's transparency,
then raised his hand,
weightless as a sigh,
across his heart,
or like a spy who examines a city map and explores:
goldfinch, lily, and river.

QUARRY

The bough bent
like a bow. Across it
an arrow of light.

—The expectancy filled
with the horde of dawn's feathers—

A lively
buzz
as of wind—and a watching
child's heart bled.

Each year the wound turns a darker red.

Itamar Ya'oz-kest   135

The flag on the house you dwelled in the wind blows now and then,
and in slow motion, like a night's passage, it leaves the mountain side.
Stretched out, impalpably, tenants wander through seventy dreams.
    The head
thrown back. With the wind moves a song of early childhood
feather-decked. Its windows lit the house is borne into
the night, to seventy semblances rolled in upon themselves,
as from the mountain side the steps of wanderers vanish.
And desolation, the mountain's scion, returns.

*   *   *

A.
A certain house buries
like a tree its fruit—
converts to root:
The father's form
like an ancient seal
the son shall bear,
and the birds above the roof
uncomprehendingly
return screaming there.

A certain house
recalls its fruit.

B.
I sit in the white light
of this house,
and gaze
at the birds on the roof
that come with spring
and leave without remembering
in fall;
the foliage of a palm tree
closes my eyes with dusky hand
and I say:
"Necromancer, do use your powers,
and raise up . . ."

136   Itamar Ya'oz-kest

and from the abyss roots rise
and I
listen for their cries:
the earth revolves
and the bones cacophonize.

C.
The hand—is the tree's,
but the cries?
Wings on the roof
or dead men's noise
in caverns of the heart;
I sit,
oh, have sat so many years
here,
in this white light,
deluding my eyes tonight. . . .
Slowly the wind buries my feet in the sand
and the walls of the house
gleam like giant monuments.

D.
The monuments
stir—
the father's head floats
in the milky light;
My Son, he calls in farewell,
you are the sacrifice,
the thicket am I.

>   In the doorway
>   he stands—
>   this father
>   won't bequeath
>   a land.

E.
—Where is the path, Father, leading home?
—My Son, the path leading home, is where?
—I'm afraid, Father, it's getting dark!

—My Son, it's getting dark and I'm afraid! . . .
—Draw me on, Father, and I'll run after you,
after you, blind
              this night———

F.
What point in my sitting here
tonight
under the star,
begging for a sign
like astrologers
—in the windows' light—
if the star is above the roof
it's equidistant
from all the ends of the world.

Is this
my house?

                              *   *   *

You build your house
by the white light of the bones. Birth
within birth sit those close to you, and a wine-glow is spread
on the table. Mother and father rise to the blessing of "Resurrector of
    the Dead"
and you move to the window to open it;
on the dunes float the scenes of your childhood:
The acacia trees bow and the birds of your hands ice-pale
strum the sunbeams amid domes and minarets.
A sleep-walking child nears and stops by the lemon blossoms
whose beauty whitens outside your window, then sits in that shade—
first dresses wounds with the bandage of a leaf, and then unbinds them.
He sleeps like the sum of your years.
The moon has stirred and the table's set.
From her apron the mother dispenses fruit that exudes a soft summer
    fragrance
while the father's hands carve the name of the place on the gate: "Bide-
    with-us!"
The child turns slowly to the meal and opens its eyes.

138   Itamar Ya'oz-kest

And you stand by the window, of your house, in the middle of the night,
and on the face of the earth
radiance and bones.

*   *   *

My father is the root in the earth,
I the tree
anxious for fruit—
birds sit at evening
on my head
tempests too
and I bend rootward.

from ORDEAL BY FIRE
(*The Bergen-Belsen Episodes*)

Railway car.
    The landscape is startled. Embarrassed
it turns its pages: tree, sky, tunnels—
(Memory=Distance+Time)
In the dark the childhood years gallop.
    And in the car the laughter of the guards collects,
    the head of a beast sprouted on the neck.

*   *   *

Suddenly a squeal.
The car has stopped;
in memory's compartment all is trapped.

*   *   *

SHOT

A bird of omen
passed—
Light! Light!
And like blood from the mouth

Itamar Ya'oz-kest   139

the darkness drains.

_____

The child gazed at the fire's flight,
and in the great heavens the moon sat sanctified.

* * *

The children called:
"Uncle, get dressed! We want
to see Death. Where is
the sickle and where is
the soul?"
Yet the man lay and as though in jest
sounded
the buzz of flies—

* * *

THE FUNERAL

The frost lashed out.
     The four winds pulled
at the hearse.
     Above the barracks sat
the magician,
    his legs folded in an X,
staring into the searchlight circles.
A treacherous wind
     halted the cart of the spirits.

Wearied beyond bearing.
     They sat down in the hearse.
The silence of ashes
    stopped the world's mouth.

ORI BERNSTEIN b. 1936

SILENT SONG

The stirrings of love alone were here.
Glasses touched one the other, like so many
crickets. All the stirrings
of love, all. A sweet fragrance
wafted about. Everyone of
them, all the stirrings.
What shook the window that wasn't
a car approaching and retreating, approaching
and retreating? A hot night,
hot night and milky
night. Till a bird's call near morning, one
bird's call within
the light, one clear bird's call, before
the approaching day.

DOG ON THE ROAD

On the road he sails like a ship
with trembling sails for limbs,
his death in the night's become a brooch
inlaid with shadows and blood.
Miraculously he's multiplied: When crushed
they took a little of him far away,
to die on lawns, in another city.
Marvelous, then, is the place of his death:

Pressed like a tree to the pavement of stone
his head brings forth large fruits of blood,
and light passes over and agitates him
like a sudden wind and death honors him
with frequent visits, to the blaring of horns.

ANOTHER TIME

Words don't express your absence.
They go their ways, as usual.
I have become a sorry mite.

Face to face I no longer converse.
Face to face I remain with you alone.
Erect the grasses cover you now.

Amid the blossoms, the spices and lights
only your mind is barrel-laden, dejected.
Surely alertness and awe are in you. In you
the courage I lost, the consolations.

Gleaming the rain covers you now.

Even from desire you broke free and here
the wind drives your face
like a large and withered leaf.

Again words overcome the eyes.

Another time stillness overcame us.

CONVERSATIONS

We used to talk a lot. Once rain
interrupted our conversation, and once hunger.
And inadvertently one of us would wander
far into the other, till frightened he'd return.

I don't know why we no longer meet.
The wind bothers you, full of seed.

From the time they stuffed you with dust like suet
you've been stopping by for brief chats.
An empty chair is filled with you in the dawn
hours, when order has gone berserk.

You go through the motions of the dead.
It's new to you. You do not fit.

Now you ask and no one answers.
A view of the earth is your share.
And the days I count already
exceed your days. And are fair.

DEPARTURE

A quiet breeze stalks
the garden I once was
and the trees tremble like a net
with a giant fish caught in it.

I must know what I shall become.
Clouds approach leisurely.
Someone has been here before me
and even his leaving remains.

Soon they will intervene. Evening
is hurled through the trees.
A bright rain shall fuse us.
And probably they meant no harm.

NOT FOR YOU

Drenched at times is your listening
With the fragrance of gardens and blessings hidden
In deep waters. Yet you are in prison.

Ori Bernstein 143

Again you're not alone. Sadness is forbidden
to enter the world lovely and smitten.
Only your trees are fall- and motion-ridden.

Inevitably the wind returns and blows.
Like a river night overtakes you. Come then, go.

YEKHI'EL KHAZAK b. 1936

ALL NIGHT LONG BURNED THE BRIDGES

All night long burned the bridges.
Without direction. To wander thus.
A white cat. And your slanted eyes.
My darling. With the loss of darkness your fabric
shall be lost. Hold on to the spinning distaff!

Dawn. The crow of the cock in a far-off yard.
The street mutters fragments of yore.
Only the wanderer wakes. Still his eyes are closed.
In the light, as in water, he bathes his face.

DALIAH RABIKOVICH b. 1936

MECHANICAL DOLL

That night I was a mechanical doll
and turned left and right, to whichever way,
and landed on my face, and broke in my fall
and they tried to piece me together artfully.

Later I resumed a patched-up rôle
and learned to refrain and obey,
but already I was a second-hand doll
like a broken branch, hanging on by a hay.

And then I went dancing at the gala ball
but they put me away with the dogs and the cats
though my steps were measured and rhythmical

And though my eyes were blue and my hair was gold
and my dress multicolored as a flowerbed
and though I wore a cherry ornament on my hat.

THE DRESS

You know, she said, they sewed you a dress of fire,
You remember how Jason's wife was burned in her dress?
It's Medea, she said, Medea did all this.
You must be careful, she said.
They sewed you a dress glowing like embers,
Burning like coals.

146

You'll wear it? She said, don't wear it.
This isn't the wind whistles but the dripping poison you hear.
You're not even a princess, what can you do to Medea?
Learn to distinguish between voices, she said,
This isn't the wind that whistles.

You remember, I told her, the time when I was six?
They washed my head with shampoo and I went out in the street.
The scent of the shampoo trailed after me like a cloud.
Then I was ill from the wind and the rain.
I still didn't know how to read Greek tragedies then,
But the fragrance spread and I was very ill.
Now I understand that the scent isn't natural.

What will become of you, she said, they sewed you a flaming dress.
They sewed me a flaming dress, I said, I know.
Then what are you waiting for, she said, be cautious,
Don't you know what a flaming dress is?

I know, I said, but not to be cautious.
That erstwhile fragrance confounds my sanity.
I told her: No one need agree with me
I don't put stock in Greek tragedies.

But the dress, she said, the dress is all afire.
What are you saying, I cried, about my attire?
I'm not wearing a dress at all, it's me who is on fire.

SURELY YOU REMEMBER

After everyone leaves
I remain alone with the poems,
some of them mine
some others' poems.
I prefer the ones that others write.
I remain quiet,
and the tension in the throat relaxes.
I remain.

Daliah Rabikovich   147

Sometimes I wish they'd all go.
Perhaps composing a poem is amusing.
You sit in the room and all the walls lengthen.
The colors turn bolder.
A blue kerchief becomes a deep well.
You wish they'd all go.
You don't know what's the matter with you.
Perhaps you'll think of two things or more.
Then it all will pass and you'll be crystal, pure.
Then will come love.
Narcissus loved himself so much.
But what fool doesn't know he also loved the river.
You sit alone.
Your heart aches but is not likely to break.
Slowly, the dim images dissolve,
then too the flaws.
Then at midnight the sun arrives
and you even recall the bleak flowers.
You wish you were dead, or alive or someone else.
Perhaps there's one land you love.
Or a single word.
Surely you remember.
What fool permits the sun to set at will.
It always hastens to wander westward towards the Isles.
To you will come sun and moon, summer and winter.
Treasures without end.

A PERSONAL OPINION

Pain is a useless thing,
I maintain,
like a worm crawling in the fruit
and the fruit ceases to be tasty.
I know you,
I can see what your youth was like
and how yellow your face has become.
It's not a story heroes spring from.

Heroes are another matter quite,
I assume,
they are nonvegetative men.
They fight in air and on sea and also in Manchuria
always in a place far-off and unusual.
My heart goes out to them, to the air, sea, and Manchuria
but they better not expect a laurel wreath.
Mostly they are to stoke engines with
as in Manchuria.
And I regret to say that they perish like dogs.

Pain is an inhuman thing
I assert,
and see no mitigating circumstance.
After all it's ugliness incarnate:
Someone lost inobtrusively
darkens progressively
darkens and rots
without a spouse and without heirs.

PORTRAIT

She sits home many a day.
She reads newspapers.
(What's the matter, don't *you* read?)
She doesn't do what she'd have liked to
she's been held back.
She craves vanilla, lots of vanilla,
give her vanilla.

In winter she's cold, really cold
colder than others are.
She dresses properly and still she's cold.
She craves vanilla.

Not that she was born yesterday, if that's what you think.
It's not the first time that she's cold.
It's not the first winter.

Daliah Rabikovich   149

Actually even the summer's unpleasant.
She reads the papers more than she'd like to.
In winter she won't budge without a stove.
She's fed up at times.
Was she asking that much of you?
Admit it, No.
She craves vanilla.

If you care to look up close, she's got a plaid skirt.
She loves a plaid skirt, thinks it cute.
To look at her, you'd laugh.
It's so ridiculous.
Even she laughs along sometimes.
It's hard for her in winter and no good in summer,
you're going to laugh,
call her mimosa,
a fowl that won't take off,
call her what you will.
She's always bundled up to stifling,
sometimes a plaid skirt plus,
you'll ask why she's bundled up to stifling?
It's a very complicated thing.
It's the cold in winter and in summer the acute heat,
never just as it should be.
And by the by, don't forget, she craves vanilla,
now she's even crying.
Give her vanilla.

HOW HONG KONG WAS DESTROYED

I'm in Hong Kong.
There's a tributary there crawling with snakes.
There's Greeks, Chinamen and blacks.
Alongside the paper lanterns carnival
crocodiles open their maws.
Who said they devour you here?

Large crowds went down to the river.
Such silk you've never seen in your life,
redder than poppy-petal red.

In Hong Kong
the sun shines in the East
and they water the flowers with a fragrant
liquid to enhance their scent.
But at night the paper lanterns toss in the wind
and when someone's murdered they ask:
Was he Chinese or black?
Did he suffer much?
And then they drop his body in the river
and all the reptiles dine.

I'm in Hong Kong,
and at night the light in the café went out.
And outside lots of paper lanterns got torn.
And the ground was erupting and seething,
erupting and seething,
and only I could tell
that there's nothing in the West
and nothing in the East.
And the paper dragon yawned
but the land erupted.
Lots of enemies will be coming here
who have never seen silk in their lives.

Only the little whores still receive their guests
in stained silk kimonos,
in tiny cubicles full of lanterns.
Some of them sob every morning
over their decaying flesh.
And if someone's killed they ask:
Oh-oh! Chinese or black?
Poor soul, hope he didn't suffer.
And at twilight already the first guests arrive
like a thorn in the living flesh.
I am in Hong Kong

Daliah Rabikovich   151

and Hong Kong is on the ocean,
hung like a colored lantern on a nail at land's end.
Perhaps the dragon
will drape it in red silk
and drop it into
the abyss of the stars.
And only the little whores will complain in their silk
that the gentlemen still
still
pinch them in their bellies.

Now I am not in Hong Kong
and Hong Kong is not on this earth.
And where Hong Kong should be
there's a single rosy spot,
half of it in heaven, the other in the sea.

YA'AKOV BESER b. 1937

SNAKE SKIN

The snake sheds its skin
to the tune of summer's flutes,
vis-á-vis a sun that assaults the naked wires
a flame-refracting emerald—
Ah, the recalcitrant
snake

drawing
death-lines across
the palm of the desert's hand.

A CHILD BUILT A CASTLE

A child
built a castle
in the sand.
Then it stopped
building.
It poured words of air
in moulds of
song.

Children
draw a house, a tree, a sky
(blue),

the leaves falling from a tree
they color
green.

But for the winds
they still haven't found
a wind-
color to use.

ALL THE CAVERNS OF LIGHT

When I traverse the distance
when I return from that distance (exclusively mine)
I come back to you. And I like to always
find you at home.
Poised and waiting

Bread crumbs all over the lines of your hands.

I wash my hands, face, clean up all the way
extend my fingers
and with their tips lift your eyes
and play with them
like a child.

Oh then
I forget all the insults I suffered,
over your body I pass on tiptoe
and find in you
all the mysteries
all the caverns of light

That illuminate
my distance, my distance to which
I return.

154   Ya'akov Beser

IN THE BEGINNING MY MOTHER SCREECHED

In the beginning
my mother screeched in the fever of coiled pain

No angel hovered above my head

Later
God created an impenetrable fog
and much rain fell
and snow
and at last the waters grew calm
and a playpen rose up and began to dissipate at once.

In kindergarten
along the river (whose name I forget)
a slide and
ladder were
ripped out
the Mickey Mouse
drawn on the wall
came down when the plaster crumbled

Quickly
they came through the garden beds
ashes
smoke-grey lizards
planted their tails in the sky.

THE SILENCE PLUCKS CHORDS

The silence plucks chords inaudibly.
A soldier lies in the last convulsion
of death;

I
have no escape from the dark of this stillness
that gnaws at the tree branches

till only a
puny trunk remains
like a shadow that melted with the molten dark.

I reach out to touch the tree
but taste
the flesh of my own fingers.
And I scream
stunned by the silence
that plucks chords inaudibly.

IT IS THE SILENCE

I come to the depths of stillness between heaven and earth to hear
how the soil returns to stone upon stone,
to the vastest silence that ever was,
the silence of chords—
touch
and they will not make a sound.

Stone upon stone,
the gaping bellies of graves,
seas deprived of their water.
The salt bleaches the bottom of lake-bowls,
in the entrails of rivers
the wind still reveres the sea
but it
       no longer
           exists . . .
You won't find submarine fragments among the stone and silt,
an ancient, worn sail maybe,
from quieter days.

The whites-of-the-eye in heaps
without a single tear's expression.

Times have changed,
no dove will soar

156 Ya'akov Beser

to fetch the bitter olive leaves.
Oh, it is the silence which lies between heaven and earth.
The troglodyte
still carves strange beasts
on ruined walls.

Oh, it is the silence which lies between heaven and earth.

MAL'AKHI BET-ARYEH b. 1937

FLESH FROM FLESH

Your velvet nakedness, in this pitch dark,
godless, you. All of me. All of you.
Vanity of the blood.
Fragrance of the flesh.

Behold a great, ominous terror descend
in this pitch darkness, your flesh before my eyes
one smoke-filled day was cloven,
flesh
and blood,
in this pitch darkness, your velvet nakedness:
your flesh—and the others'

YA'IR HURVITS b. 1941

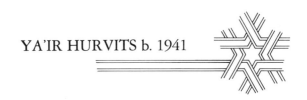

FOR MY LOVE RISING EARLY

Silent, silent evening passes
through tree and heart. The earth
abandons its face to the sky's blessing and the wind
exhaling cold scatters
the darkening magic in turning leaves and heralds
for aspiring seedlings the coming
of water to thirsting roots. Silent

Silent in my love. Return
return to your enchantment, my love, return
in the guise of an angel's face, an angel's face, my love.
On islands angels recline and stalk
the bursting light of flowers, in their delight floating
invisible on the seas,
and only the heart implants jealousy in these angels reclining
on islands, by islands evening

Passes silent, silent, the earth
abandons its face and the breeze will blow the clear air briskly for my
    love
rising early.

ON A CLEAR NIGHT

the earth conceived and in windows
wind-blown birds

159

fret the leaves with their sad wanderings. In my yard
a bird gathers dead grass from a dead ground,
revives
        to warm in sleepy vessels
both feathers and water. Now in the gardens,
approaching her night,
the softly conversing fishes in their hiding, the star in their eye, she
    dreams
of the purple gates and from her wings
the shards of dawn hoard many suns, and glisten
on broken rocks.

Slowly the winds of forgetfulness stir.
Leaflessness naps in the tips of the birds.

The bird constructs the sky with her light, distills
a pure warmth onto the light,
her festival fruit, kindling bluish in its pool
out of the seeds' darkness. I dream
of the broken rock surfacing from water,
espy the rivulets
on a clear night.

SORROW MY LOVE

Sorrow my love, soon my life, soon
I and my death like a blossom
shall unfold and the dog come to the quicksands and say:

The keeper of the garden reserves my soul for love.
In the garden of the soul there'll be weeping,
bushes and birds shall lament all about
for sorrow is my love. Phantoms stalk

There. A shade is my love.
Bless, my soul, bless the bridal bird
nesting in the clouds. Night
still. The sun reclines on the vital waters.

160   Ya'ir Hurvits

Kindling shall I light
in the void.

Mist is its shroud.
My own sweetness craves the tranquillity of leaves.

ME'IR WIESELTIER b. 1941

TAKE POEMS, BUT DON'T READ

Take poems, but don't read
use this book violently:
Spit on it, squash it
kick it, pinch it.

Toss this book in the ocean
to see whether it can swim.
Hold it over the gas flame
to see whether it's fireproof.
Nail it, saw it
to see whether it has resistance:

This book is a rag made of paper
with letters like flies, whereas you
you rag of flesh, who eats dust and bleeds,
you puzzle drowsily over it.

I SHALL EMPTY MY HEAD LIKE JAM . . .

I shall empty my head like jam with a spoon.
I shall become a jar with smeared sides.
I shall put me in the sun to dry.
Dried I shall be, something fruit-like.

+30° C

Snow falls
on the contraption
snow falls
ceaselessly
at night
in June
what peace
snow falls
across the keys
the deer of the north
wag their heads
snow falls
into its entrails
the letter "a"
is already
out of sight
on fingers
snow
melts
like tears
white snow
wise
banal
innocent lamb
as in stories
for children
snow
falls and the ceiling
is a cloud
traveling
transporting
the snow
out of here
to another place
only the contraption

Me'ir Wieseltier   163

is still
sunk in it
if the snow melts
it will melt in it.

THE WEATHER

Rain falls in Tel Aviv on a June morning;
right before my eyes yet imperceptibly.
On the dark trees and the battered houses of Reinës Street
a rain that consoles like a children's dream in bed.

And the faces are wet with blessing and the lips mutter,
and the graded light comes, leans on the edge of the houses.
In the eyes a thousand years lie like yesterday,
and yesterday seeps into the weathered walls.

Have a rash love unleash like an allergic arm's rash
when the nectar of figs is on the tongue and pricks the palate—
the flesh speaks out like a telephone
and through the body trickles an imaginary rain.

FRIENDS

Friends come and talk; they talk and you talk
and eight, ten, fourteen
eyes range tremulously, despairing, tiny flies
in their quest for honey, jam
something sweet, taffy for the soul.

They sit and rise and drink with age-old hope,
and the soul whose sap has drained yearns to be sweet;
someone gives you a look as though he gave you a note:

And you slip the note in your pocket and return a look to put things
right.
And he nods as though it were now possible to speak, and you no longer
need to write.

164   Me'ir Wieseltier

—AND EVEN IF THEY LIVE . . .

—-And even if they live a thousand years,
the men will consider the women they clasp chattel,
and the women the men they clasp chattel,
and the children they bear chattel,
and the children the parents who feed them chattel:
For these people
drift from acquisition to acquisition.

And they bury like one who buries a treasure in the earth,
and stand weeping because they can no longer
raise a hand and grab: For these people
have grasping hands.

CAUTION PREVENTS ACCIDENTS

Cautiously the sun shone on the damp sand.
Cautiously the leaves began to shake off the dews of night.
Cautiously the man placed the pajama tops and bottoms on the chair.
Cautiously the first busses darted to the terminal.
Cautiously the paper boy aimed the rolled-up sheet.
Cautiously the children conversed on their way to school.
Cautiously the heavy doors of the banks opened.
Cautiously one hundred thousand clerks sipped from their first tea.
Cautiously the Prime Minister convened with the Minister of Defense.
Cautiously the postman dropped off envelope after envelope.
Cautiously the harbor cranes wagged their tips above the boat.
Cautiously the housewife selected the lovely fruit.
Cautiously the Minister of Defense briefed the Air Force Commander.
Cautiously the pupils removed their bicycles from the rack.
Cautiously the greengrocer maneuvered between the fruit and the bee.
Cautiously the man ducked under the parasols of the café.
Cautiously the lifeguard counted the heads in the water.
Cautiously the neighbor placed her folding table on the porch.
Cautiously the Air Force Commander phoned the Commander of the
    Base.

Me'ir Wieseltier   165

Cautiously the line outside the movie house box office grew.
Cautiously the couple picked the furniture out from the window display.
Cautiously the lights went on each after the other in the street.
Cautiously the woman gathered the wash from the line.
Cautiously the trembling youth fondled his girlfriend's breasts.
Cautiously the city lights played across the expanse of darkening water.
That night, stray shots were fired on the border
which were answered by stray lines in the morning papers. No one
was hurt.
A strange quiet like that we haven't known in ages.

APPENDIX: NOTES ON THE POETS

Had John Ciardi's assertion that one can be a poet only in the language in which one first said, "Mama!" been true, there would have been no modern Hebrew poetry. As the following notes show, the majority of the poets were not born in Israel and acquired Hebrew as a second language. Yekhi'el Mar began writing poetry in German. He came to Palestine when he was sixteen-and-a-half. Of the transition he said: "When I came to the country, after three months, even less, I began to sense the language. Not so much know it, but to sense it and to open up to its beauty. . . . Two years passed, and I began to write."

Where problems exist in spelling the poets' names I have offered the variants in parentheses. The differences stem partly from choices in notation. Amichai, for example, seemed to me misleading; Amihai not good enough—the *kh* sound (as in the German word *nach*) does not exist in English, but the exact pronunciation requires it: Amikhai. Even within the Hebrew, variants occur because the vowel-points are not always given, and different books use different forms. Thus one will find Tan'ee and Tanai, Ratosh and Ratush. Israel Efrat was formerly called, according to the Ashkenazy pronunciation, Israel Efros.

Finally, when the poets had European names which were transcribed into Hebrew and had now to be retranscribed into the English, I found myself with an embarrassment of riches: Tuvia Rübner in the Hebrew is transcribed as Rivner or Ribner; Esther Raab as Rab or Rav, or even Raav.

In the case of first names I generally chose the Hebrew rather than the English version: Mosheh for Moses, Gavri'el rather than Gabriel, and Shlomoh instead of Solomon. I drew the line, however, at Benjamin, Ben-Zion and Esther—Benyamin, Ben-Tsi'on and Ester looked too odd and were close enough to the English pronunciation not to require substitution.

ALTERMAN, NATAN. 1910–70. Born in Warsaw, Alterman immigrated to Palestine in 1925; he studied in the Gymnasium Hertzliyah in Tel Aviv. He served on the newspaper staff of *Ha-Arets* (1934–43) and of the *Davar* (from 1943 on). His satirical "Seventh Column" in the *Davar* became popular. His poetic works include

Paupers' Joy (1944) and *City of the Dove* (1957). He translated both Racine and Shakespeare.

AMIKHAI (Amichai, Amihai), YEHUDAH. 1924– . Born in Würzburg, Germany, Amikhai came to Palestine in 1936. He served in the British army during World War II, and later in the Israeli army. He studied at Hebrew University in Jerusalem and teaches literature now in high school. His poetic works include *Now and in Days of Yore* (1955), and *Time* (1977). He has also written short stories and a novel.

AMIR, AHARON. 1923– . Born in Kovno, Lithuania, Amir came to Palestine in 1935. He studied at the Gymnasium Hertzliyah in Tel Aviv and Hebrew University in Jerusalem. His works include the poetry volume *Peg* (1970), the novel *And Death Shall Have No Dominion* (1955), and *Love,* a collection of short stories.

AVIDAN, DAVID. 1934– . Avidan was born in Tel Aviv and studied at Hebrew University in Jerusalem. He worked as journalist on the paper *Yedi'ot Akhronot,* and it was in newspapers that he began publishing in 1950. His poetic works include *Something for Someone* (1964) and *External Poems* (1970). His volume *Impossible Poems* caused a furor because of its unorthodoxy. He has also written a play, *The End of the Season Is the End of the World.*

BAT-MIRIAM, YOKHEVED. 1901– . Born in Russia, Bat-Miriam studied at the Universities of Odessa and Moscow. She came to Palestine in 1928 and has published since 1922. Her best known volume is the *Ghetto Poems* (1943).

BEN-AMITTAI, LEVI. 1901– . Born in Russia, Ben-Amittai joined the Pioneer group in 1917 and came to Palestine in 1920. He worked on construction, then joined the *kvutsah* or commune of Deganya, where he taught until 1939. His first poems were published in newspapers in 1925. His poetic works include *Nights under Siege* (1937) and *The Fields That in the Valley* (1940).

BERNSTEIN, ORI. 1936– . Born in Tel Aviv, Bernstein studied law at Hebrew University in Jerusalem. He served in the Israeli army as military defense counsel and later practiced law in Tel Aviv. He has published since 1953, and his works include *In the Same Room, In the Same Light* (poetry, 1962) and *The Waters Flowing Counterwise* (short stories, 1959).

BESER, YA'AKOV. 1937– . Beser came to Israel as an adolescent. His poetic works include *Winter Nineteen Forty* . . . (1965), *In the Tangle of Roots* (1967), and *Field for Stoning* (1973).

BET-ARYEH, MAL'AKHI. 1937– . Israeli born, educated in Ramat Gan and Hebrew University in Jerusalem, Bet-Aryeh now works at the Division of Hebrew Writings in Jerusalem. His first poems appeared in periodicals. He has also written prose and children's literature (*Why Did the Sun Disappear?* 1960).

BIALIK, KHAYIM NAKHMAN. 1873–1934. Bialik was born in Volhnia, Russia. In 1891 he came to Odessa, where he published his first poem. He came to Palestine in 1924 and founded Dvir, the publishing company of which he became editor. In addition to his voluminous poetic oeuvre he wrote short stories and translated Cervantes's *Don Quixote* and Schiller's *Wilhelm Tell* into Hebrew. He died on a trip to Austria, and his body was brought back to Palestine for burial.

CHERNIKHOVSKY (Tchernichovsky), SHA'UL. 1875–1943. Born in the Crimea, Russia, Chernikhovsky received a secular education and went to Germany to study medicine. He settled in Palestine in 1931, where he continued to write and practice medicine. In addition to his poetry he translated many of the classics, including Homer, Molière and Shakespeare.

DOR, MOSHEH. 1932– . Born in Tel Aviv, Dor was educated both there and at Hebrew University in Jerusalem. As a journalist he served on the staff of the *Ma'ariv*. He is now Israel's counselor for cultural affairs in London. First published in periodicals in 1948, Dor's works include the poetry volume *Gold and Dust* (1963) and translations of G. K. Chesterton, E. Bentley, and Doyle.

EFRAT (Efros), ISRAEL. 1891– . Born in Volhnia, Russia, Efrat immigrated to the United States in 1905. He studied at Columbia University and taught at the University of Buffalo 1929–41 and Hunter College 1941–55. Moving to Israel in 1955, he served as rector at the University of Tel Aviv. He began publishing in 1912 and has translated some of Bialik's work into English. His most recent volume of poetry is *Elul Is a Month All Song* (1971).

ELDAN, ANADAD. 1924– . Born in Poland, Eldan came to Palestine in 1930. He grew up in the commune of Kheftsi-Bah and remained a member there until 1960. He has since joined a *kibuts* in the Negev. His poems first appeared in 1953, and his poetic work includes *Darkness Flows in the Fruit* (1960), *With Joys Not Lightly* (1964), and *Internal Light* (1973).

GALAI, BENJAMIN. 1921– . Born in Russia, Galai came to Palestine at the age of five and was educated in Tel Aviv. He served in the British air force during World War II. Since 1962 he has been active in journalism. His poetic works include *On Compassion's Shore* (1958) and *Journey to the North* (1968).

GAR, TSFRIRAH. 1924– . Gar has published *The Sunflower Circle* (1966) and *Spot on the Sun* (1970).

GILBO'A, AMIR. 1917– . Born in Volhnia, Gilbo'a came to Palestine in 1937 and served in the British army during World War II. He began publishing his work in 1941. His poetry volumes include *Poems in the Morning, in the Morning* (1953), *Blues and Reds* (1964), *To Write the Lips of the Sleeping I Desired* (1968), and *Gazelle, I Send You* (1972).

GOLDBERG, LE'AH. 1911–70. Born in Kovno, Lithuania, Goldberg learned Hebrew there. In 1930 she went to study at the University of Berlin and later Bonn. She came to Palestine in 1935 where she joined the newspaper staff first of the *Davar* and later *Ha-Mishmar*. She joined the faculty of Hebrew University in Jerusalem in 1954 as lecturer on comparative literature. Her poetic works include *Morning Glory* (1955) and *Early and Late* (1959).

GREENBERG (Grünberg), URI TSVI. 1894– . Born in Galicia,

Greenberg served in the Austrian army during World War I. He came to Palestine in 1924, where he joined a work camp. He joined the newspaper *Davar* when it was founded. His poetic works include *House Dog* (1929) and *River Roads* (1951).

GURI (Gouri), KHAYIM. 1922– . Born in Tel Aviv, Guri studied agriculture. He was active in the Israeli Liberation War and later studied at Hebrew University in Jerusalem and at the Sorbonne. He first published his work in 1943. His poetic works include *Till Dawn Come* (1959) and *Rose of the Winds* (1960).

HA-ME'IRI (formerly Feuerstein), AVIGDOR. 1890–1970. Born in Russia, Ha-Me'iri received a religious upbringing. He studied in Budapest and was active in the Zionist Youth Movement. He participated in the Zionist Congress of 1913 in Vienna. During World War I he served as officer in the Hungarian army and, when captured, was sent to Siberia. With the Russian Revolution he was freed and came to Kiev and then Odessa. He arrived in Palestine in 1921, where he lived first in Tel Aviv and later in Ramat Gan. A posthumous selection of his poems, *A Collection of Poems,* came out in 1976.

HURVITS (Hurvitz, Hourvitz), YA'IR. 1941– . Born in Tel Aviv, Hurvits is the author of *Poems for Louise* (1964), *Season of the Witch* (1970), *Narcissi for the Mud Kingdom* (1973), and *Sitting by Myself* (1976). He is a member of the editorial board of the *Siman Kri'a* literary quarterly.

KHALFI (Chalfi, Halfi), AVRAHAM. 1904– . Born in Lodz, Poland, Khalfi was educated in the Ukraine and became an actor there. In Palestine (1924) he worked first in agriculture and then joined the "Ohel" theatre upon its founding in 1925. In 1953 he went over to the "Te'atron Cameri." His work was first published in 1933. His volumes of poetry include *Across from Stars and Dust* (1962) and *In the Shade of Every Place* (1970).

KHAZAK (Chazak, Hazak), YEKHI'EL. 1936– . Born in Israel, Khazak was raised in a *kibuts* and became active in agriculture. He first published his work in 1959 in *Ha-Keshet*. Some of his poems are collected in *Basalt Rocks* (1961).

KHOMSKY (Chomsky, Homsky), DOV. 1913–76. Khomsky was born in Minsk, Russia, but went to live in Poland after World War I. He later studied at the Hebrew Seminar in Vilna. Coming to Palestine in 1936, he studied at Hebrew University in Jerusalem and then taught. After serving in World War II, he became a school principal in Tel Aviv. His publications include the poetry volumes *Desert Songs* (1947), *On the Road* (1951), and *Till the Moon Set* (1975).

KOVNER, ABBA. 1918– . Born in Sevastopol, Russia, Kovner grew up in Vilna, where he was active in the youth movement "Ha-Shomer Ha-Tsa'ir." He was a partisan leader when the Germans took over Vilna. He came to Palestine in 1945, and his first poems were published in the newspaper *Ha-Arets* in 1943, smuggled over from Vilna by partisan mail. His poetic works include *Land of Sand* (1961), *Of All Those Loves* (1965), and *Observations* (1977).

MAR, YEKHI'EL. 1921–69. Born in Poland, Mar came to Palestine in 1937 with the Youth Aliyah. He was raised in a *kibuts*. In 1948 he served in the Israeli army and lived thereafter in Tel Aviv. His poetic works include *Lines to the Circle* (1957), *Handful of Wind* (1962), and *New Poems* (1965).

NETSER (Netzer), ELI. 1933– . Born in Budapest, Netser came to Israel in 1949 and served in the Israeli army. He joined *kibuts* Dalyah. His poetic works include *Almond in the Rain* (1961) and *The Hungry Keep Awake All Night* (1963).

OFFEN, YEHUDAH. 1922– . Born in Germany, Offen was educated in Kiel and Hamburg. In 1938 he was deported to Poland and in 1939 succeeded in immigrating to Palestine, where he served in the British army. He worked in agriculture, diamond cutting, and journalism. His poems began appearing in periodicals in 1950, and his poetic works include *Without Destination* (1961) and *Mountain and Militance* (1963).

PAGIS (Paggis), DAN. 1930– . Born in Bukovina, Pagis was raised in Vienna and spent World War II in a concentration camp. He came to Palestine in 1947 and joined *kibuts* Merkhavyah. Later he taught high school in Jerusalem while studying at Hebrew University. He is now professor of medieval literature at the university. His poetic works include *Sun Dial* (1959), *Belated Spare Time* (1964), and *Brain* (1977).

PREIL, GAVRI'EL. 1911– . Born in Estonia, Preil studied at the university in Latvia. He came to the United States in 1922 and has studied at Yeshiva University in New York City. His first publication was in the Palestinian newspaper *Ha-Do'ar*. His poetic works include *Landscapes of Sun and Frost* and *Candle Next to the Stars* (1954). He also writes in Yiddish and English and has translated some of the Hebrew poets into English.

RAAB (Rab, Raav, Rav), ESTHER. 1899– . Born in Petakh Tikvah, Palestine, Raab lived in Deganyah and, after her marriage, in Egypt (1920–25). Later she returned to Tel Aviv and Petakh Tikvah. Her poetic works include *The Poems of Esther Raab* (1963) and *Last Prayer* (1972).

RABIKOVICH (Ravikovich), DALIAH. 1936– . Born in Ramat Gan, Palestine, Rabikovich studied at Hebrew University in Jerusalem. She now lives in Tel Aviv. Her poetic works include *The Love of an Orange* (1963), *Difficult Winter* (1964), and *The Third Book* (1970).

RATOSH (Ratush, formerly Halpern), YONATAN. 1909– . Born in Warsaw, Ratosh came to Palestine as a child and went to the Gymnasium Hertzliyah for his schooling. He later studied law and went to Paris to study philology. His first poems appeared in 1925 in the newspaper *Ha-Arets*. His poetic works include *Black Canopy* (1941), *Rib* (1959), *Mathematical Poems* (1963), and *Concrete Poems* (1965).

ROKE'AKH (Roke'ah), DAVID, 1916– . Born in Lvov, Roke'akh came to Palestine in 1934 and worked there as an architect. His first poems were published the following year. His poetic works include *From Summer to Summer* (1964) and *Eyes to the Rock* (1967).

Appendix: Notes on the Poets   173

RÜBNER (Rivner, Ribner), TUVIA. 1924– . Born in Czechoslovakia, Rübner came to Palestine in 1941 and joined *kibuts* Merkhavyah. He fought in the Israeli army and now teaches at the *kibuts*. He wrote at first in German but published his first Hebrew poems in 1953. His poetic works include *The Fire in the Stone* (1957) and *Songs for Finding Time* (1961).

SADEH, PINKHAS. 1929– . Born in Lvov, Sadeh came to Palestine in 1934 and grew up in *kibuts* Sarid. He studied in London. His first poems came out in 1945. In addition to poetry, he also writes children's books.

SHALOM, SHIN (pseud. for Shalom Shapiro; sometimes written Sh. Shalom). 1904– . Born in Poland, Shalom came to Palestine in 1922 and settled in Jerusalem. He studied at Erlangen University in Germany (1930–31) and taught Hebrew literature in Jerusalem until 1939. He now lives in Haifa. His oeuvre: *The Collected Works of Shin Shalom* (1966).

SHATAL, SHMU'EL. 1913– . Born in Pinsk, Poland, Shatal came to Palestine in 1929; he is an architect. His work was first published in 1938, and his volume *Chords to the Stone* appeared in 1964.

SHLONSKY, AVRAHAM. 1900–73. Born in the Ukraine, Shlonsky came to Palestine in 1912, studied at Gymnasium Hertzliyah, and then returned to the Ukraine. In 1921 he immigrated and settled in Tel Aviv. His *Poems,* in two volumes, appeared in 1954. He has translated Molière, Shakespeare, and Pushkin into Hebrew.

SHNE'UR (Schneour), ZALMAN. 1886–1959. Born in Russia, Shne'ur came to Odessa when he was fifteen; there Bialik encouraged his literary ambitions. His work first appeared in an adult publication in 1902. In 1924 he went to live in Paris, where he remained until World War II. In 1941 he moved to the United States, and in 1951 he settled in Israel. His poetic works include *At Sunset* (1907) and *Songs and Poems* (1914); the collected *Poems* appeared in two volumes in 1958.

TAN'EE (Tanai), SHLOMOH. 1919– . Tan'ee came to Palestine when he was nine years old and was educated in Rekhovot and Tel Aviv. He traveled to France in 1947 and to the United States in 1952. He is a member of the staff of the paper *Ha-Arets,* and his first publication appeared in 1938. His poetic works include *Land of the Living* (1955), *Stars of the Road* (1956), and *Selected Poems* (1961).

TOMER, BEN-ZION. 1928– . Born in Poland, Tomer fled to Russia with the outbreak of World War II. In 1943 he came to Palestine with a youth group. During the Liberation War he was taken prisoner in Jordan; on his return he studied at Hebrew University in Jerusalem and also in Europe. Some of his poems were collected in *The River Returns* (1959) and his play, *Phantoms* (1963), was staged by the *Ha-Bimah.*

TRAININ (Treinin), AVNER. 1928– . Born in Tel Aviv, Trainin studied chemistry at Hebrew University in Jerusalem and in Cambridge, England. At present he is professor of chemistry at Hebrew University. His poetry appeared in *The Moss of the Wall* (1957).

WIESELTIER, ME'IR. 1941– . Born in Moscow, Wieseltier now lives in Tel Aviv. His poetic work includes *Chapter One, Chapter Two* (1967) and *Take!* (1973).

WINKLER, M(ANFRED). 1922– . Born in Rumania, Winkler came to Israel in 1959 and has worked as archivist and editor. His poetic volumes include *Poems* (1965) and *Between the Fingers of Poetry* (1970).

YALAN-SHTEKLIS, MIRIAM. 1900– . Born in Russia and educated first in Berlin and then at the University of Kharkov, Yalan-Shteklis came to Palestine in 1920. She initially wrote poetry in Russian and later in German and Yiddish, as well as in Hebrew. She has also written many children's poems.

YA'OZ-KEST, ITAMAR. 1934– . Born in Hungary, Ya'oz-Kest was deported to Bergen Belsen in 1944. He came to Israel in 1951 and studied at the Hebrew University in Jerusalem. He continued to write in

Hungarian for some time before commencing to write his poems in Hebrew. His poetic works include *Angel without Wings* (1959), *Landscape under Smoke* (1961), and *Poems* (1966).

ZELDA (full name: ZELDA MISHKOVSKY). 1914– . Her poetic works include *Time: Poems* (1967) and *Don't Be Distant* (1975).